Mildret Araya

A CULTURAL HISTORY OF SPANISH AMERICA

A CULTURAL HISTORY
OF SPANISH AMERICA

From Conquest to Independence

BY MARIANO PICÓN-SALAS

TRANSLATED BY IRVING A. LEONARD

UNIVERSITY OF CALIFORNIA PRESS

Berkeley, Los Angeles, London | 1971

UNIVERSITY OF CALIFORNIA PRESS

BERKELEY AND LOS ANGELES, CALIFORNIA

UNIVERSITY OF CALIFORNIA PRESS, LTD.

LONDON, ENGLAND

© 1962 BY THE REGENTS OF THE UNIVERSITY OF CALIFORNIA

TRANSLATED FROM *DE LA CONQUISTA A LA INDEPENDENCIA.*
TRES SIGLOS DE HISTORIA CULTURAL HISPANOAMERICANA
(MÉXICO, FONDO DE CULTURA ECONÓMICA, 1944; 2D ED. REV., 1950; 3D ED., 1958)

Published with the assistance of a grant from the Ford Foundation

ISBN: 0-520-01012-4

LIBRARY OF CONGRESS CATALOG CARD NUMBER: 62-15381

SIXTH PRINTING, 1971

MANUFACTURED IN THE UNITED STATES OF AMERICA

Translator's Foreword

The story of Hispanic America is often told in terms of the drama of the Spanish Conquest, the wars for independence, and the rise and fall of dictatorships, when the illusion of popular sovereignty had replaced the absolutism of the Spanish kings. Writers of history, perhaps wishing to enliven their pages, have often stressed sensational events and personalities in their narratives, and this procedure has tended to promote the notion that history is politics and military conflict. Even a more recent shift of emphasis to economic and social aspects falls short of giving the fullest comprehension of the complex nature of the southern lands and peoples of the Western Hemisphere. Another useful approach is "cultural history," of which the book by Professor Picón-Salas is an excellent example.

It has been said that character is destiny, that is, history. If so, what are the basic factors which, in common with the rest of mankind, have conditioned the historical evolution of Spanish American peoples? What are the fundamental determinants of their character? Briefly, they are heredity and environment which interweave, like the warp and woof of cloth, to form the fabric of personality. Varying heredity and environment produce varied cultural patterns, and it is well at once to reject valuations of superior and inferior and to concentrate on the particular manifestations that Hispanic America offers. But, although geography is the setting in which the drama of human history unfolds and its importance should not be minimized (though it is fashionable to discount "geographical determinism"),

Professor Picón-Salas's study is almost exclusively concerned with the "perpendicular" thread of heredity rather than with the "horizontal" thread of environment. This, however, is not necessarily a weakness, for he has skillfully addressed himself to the difficult task of identifying and weighing the more impalpable factors of inheritance that have formed the character and personality of present-day Spanish America. If, indeed, heredity may be defined as accumulated past environment, that is, the sum total of the reactions of successive generations to the same or similar conditions, a discussion limited to the hereditary background of our hemispheric neighbors can contribute much to our understanding of them. In this effort Professor Picón-Salas has succeeded notably by providing a much-needed, and thus far the best, synthesis of the colonial heritage whose influence in shaping the modern mind of the peoples "south of the border" is still underestimated and too little understood.

An assessment of what seems the remote past of Spanish America is conceivably of greater utility for a comprehension of today's problems than an account of more recent history. The colonial heritage of these southern regions was the work of several centuries and differed fundamentally from that of North America. Spanish America's colonial formation lasted a full three hundred years which is approximately twice as long as its separate, politically independent existence. This period of European tutelage was also about twice as long as that of the English colonies along the Atlantic that coalesced into the United States. Although this longer time certainly made for a greater hardening of the Hispanic American pattern, it is less important than the peculiar nature of the culture that was fixed upon nearly two-thirds of the Western Hemisphere during those three centuries.

Spain and Portugal moved westward to form eventually a larger Spain and a larger Portugal about one hundred and fifteen years before England followed the same course to establish a larger England. Columbus began the first migration in 1492 while the earliest English settlement at Jamestown came almost six score years later in 1607. This span of time witnessed a rapid transition from the medieval to the modern age with its extraordinary changes in spiritual, intellectual, economic, and social values that were reflected in the differing cultural patterns of Anglo-America and Hispanic America.

The Europe that Columbus left behind at the close of the fifteenth century still retained some uniformity and solidarity of life and spirit. No clear sense of nationality had emerged anywhere, and the medieval dream of universal empire, symbolized in the Holy Roman Empire, lingered on. Throughout the Continent the structure of society remained essentially feudal with a small aristocracy reposing on a vast pedestal of peasant serfs, though fissures and cracks, to be sure, were discernible in many areas and a small middle class existed in the large towns and cities. Whether in England, Germany, France, Italy, or Spain, the same general outline of feudal organization was recognizable, and the variations seemed unimportant. In an age when religion was the dominant preoccupation, the universality of Catholic Christianity appeared assured, for the Protestant revolt was still in the future. Intellectually all parts of western Europe accepted theology and philosophy as the highest expression of mental activity and the only valid approach to ultimate truth. Learning everywhere was authoritarian and scholastic, and Latin was its universal medium; experimentalism and modern science had not yet advanced far enough to threaten old certainties. Under such auspices Hispanic America began.

In the one hundred and fifteen years from the first voyage of Columbus to the settlement at Jamestown, knowledge of the physical and intellectual world of Europe had expanded enormously. The little, tight Mediterranean world had exploded into a spherical globe of unimagined dimensions. The Ptolemaic universe, with the earth its center and pivotal point, had yielded to the Copernican universe, with the earth a mere peripheral planet of an immense solar system. Europe's physical, intellectual, and spiritual solidarities were fast melting away. In vague contours a pattern of conflicting nationalisms was emerging, the generalized feudal structure was disintegrating, particularly in the more northerly parts, and a more vigorous middle class was undermining the power and influence of the aristocracy. An aggressive financial capitalism was competing with the earlier agrarian capitalism, and the Lutheran schism divided the universal Church into two hostile factions, the Protestant North and the Cath-

olic South. In this great cultural crisis Spain chose to maintain orthodoxy in social, intellectual, and religious matters by crushing dissension. A neoscholasticism combatted developing science, and doctrine
after doctrine in both natural and moral philosophy were withdrawn
from the possibility of rational proof and relegated to the sphere of
unquestioned dogma. Faith transcended Reason in all things. The
efforts of Catholic Spain and Portugal to preserve the old unchanged
were zealously extended to their overseas possessions where a large
subject population of sedentary Indians and mixed elements facilitated the continuance of the feudal social structure visibly declining
in Europe. Thus a medieval civilization, revering intellectual and
spiritual as well as political authority, acquired a new lease of life
and became the heritage of modern Hispanic America.

English settlers, who were already the beneficiaries of the shifting
from a feudalistic society, from a purely agrarian capitalism, and
from a completely authoritarian learning, reached North America
more than a century after the Spaniards and found there no Indian
labor to exploit. Circumstances required self-reliance, new attitudes,
and flexible patterns which helped to create a dynamic heritage contrasting with the relatively static heritage of the longer-established
Spanish Americans. It is this latter patrimony that is brilliantly described and analyzed in the pages which follow.

Professor Mariano Picón-Salas is a Venezuelan prose writer of
great distinction and a Spanish American master of the essay, a literary form more widely and successfully cultivated in his part of the
world today than in the United States. He is, moreover, a versatile
writer with numerous short stories and novels to his credit, including
Viaje al amanecer (Journey to the Dawn), Registro de huéspedes
(Guest Register), Odisea de Tierra Firme (Mainland Odyssey), and
Los tratos de la noche (Night Deals); also, in illuminating biographies he evokes with scholarly imagination the lives of the precursor
of Spanish American independence, Francisco de Miranda, and of
a saintly protector of Negro slaves in colonial New Granada, Pedro
Claver. The history of literature and of the fine arts has claimed the
attention of his pen, but possibly its most impressive products are
his broadly based cultural and sociological studies of which De la

conquista a la independencia is, perhaps, the finest. His most recent book is the autobiographical *Regreso de tres mundos* (Return from Three Worlds) which admirably combines ideas and incidents of his own generation with historical and cultural events in Venezuela and Chile during the first three decades of this century. A respect for esthetic canons, together with a mild scepticism and an absence of doctrinaire attitudes, underlie all his mature writings. A modest, even-tempered man, he writes with a warmth tinged with gentle irony and wit. Light rather than heat emerges from his discussions.

His career is even more varied than his works. Born in 1901 to a comfortable, middle-class family in the highland city of Mérida, situated in the picturesque surroundings of the Andes, where the rhythm of life in a community that had barely entered the money economy seemed nearly as calm and unruffled as in the eighteenth century. Changing times made that residence the lost Eden of his childhood, for they reduced the family to near bankruptcy. An avid reader, he became a precocious intellectual, and his opposition to the Venezuelan despot Juan Vicente Gómez, brought exile in Chile. The precarious economic existence of Picón-Salas in that hospitable land did not prevent a pursuit of knowledge in its national university where, in 1928, he received a doctorate in philosophy and letters and where he served as a professor until 1936. The death of the tyrant Gómez in 1935 permitted a return to Venezuela to hold various offices in the Ministry of Education. Since 1936 the political vicissitudes of his country have made him alternately a roving professor abroad and a diplomatic representative of Venezuela but consistently a writer of increasing maturity. With various commissions he has moved about Europe, the United States, Mexico, and South America. It was while serving as a Visiting Professor at Columbia University, Smith College, and Middlebury College from 1942 to 1944 that he shaped the material that went into *From Conquest to Independence*. In 1946 and 1947 he served as Dean of the School of Education of the Central University at Caracas. From 1949 to 1951 he taught at the University of Puerto Rico, College of Mexico, and at the University of California, Los Angeles. Meanwhile he filled diplomatic posts, including that of ambassador of Venezuela to Colombia

(1947–1948) and to Brazil (1958–1959). In 1959 he became a permanent delegate of Venezuela to UNESCO in Paris.

It is singularly opportune that *De la conquista a la independencia* becomes available to the English-speaking world, and particularly to the public in the United States, at a time when the latter country is at last addressing itself to the fundamental problems of Hispanic America. To appreciate the gravity of this undertaking and to understand its difficulties, the people of the United States need to acquaint themselves with the potent past of our southern neighbors. Few works in any language deal so lucidly and cogently with this past of Spanish America that is so closely related to the present as this survey of Professor Picón-Salas. Written with the dispassionate objectivity of a cosmopolitan South American but with a warmth of feeling, it is immensely useful to enhance the understanding of a North American audience. The fact that it has run through several editions in its original Spanish attests to its acceptance by the public of Hispanic America. Especially helpful are the penetrating chapters on the baroque seventeenth century, the period of consolidation of Hispanic civilization that has left so indelible an imprint on the Spanish American character. If one may quibble now and then about a minor detail as, for instance, the conventional treatment of the Inquisition, or the alleged noncirculation of imported books of light literature and secular nonfiction in the former colonies, such flaws are hardly discernible amidst the merits of this admirable synthesis of the cultural heritage of Spanish America. This work contains much information; more importantly, it provides understanding.

IRVING A. LEONARD

Heathbrook,
South Tamworth (East Sandwich), N.H.,

Preface

From the large and complex subject of the colonial history of Spanish America, which has not yet been investigated or interpreted in any definitive manner, I have ventured to select a few topics that, in the synthetic form our busy times demand, will offer the clearest image I am able to give of the formative process of our Creole or Spanish American character. How this Hispanic American culture was shaped, what intellectual and spiritual ingredients went into it, what European elements underwent a change in migrating to the New World, and which ones grew out of the *mestizo* or hybrid spirit —these are some of the questions to which this essay in cultural history seeks to address itself. The book is based on a number of courses given at colleges and universities of the United States, including the Hispanic Department of Columbia University, Smith College at Northampton, Massachusetts, and summer sessions at Middlebury, Vermont, in 1942 and 1943. To make the work readable, and not limited to a respected but small group of experts, I have pruned it of scholarly impedimenta or of strictly pedagogical matter which the more serious student may restore and extend by consulting suitable bibliographies. The university world of the United States is so well established, compact, and rich in resources that it tends to induce and at times to overesteem an excess of erudition that obscures by exhaustive documentation the human and sensitive side inherent in every worthwhile study. This tendency reaches a point, indeed—and this is a real danger in modern universities—at which one merely writes for other scholars or to accumulate a list of publications for academic advancement. Therefore there are kinds of *idola universitatis* that Francis Bacon never knew, and there are works so erudite that the thoroughness of the research eliminates the personality and feeling of the scholar. And so, in accordance with my temperament, I am more concerned with what is genuinely typical than with a vast amount of data; and, rather than burden the text with footnotes and citations, I prefer what reveals not only an effort to convey information but what, from the human point of view, is more urgent—that is, to *understand* it.

In offering these pages to the public, I recall with pleasure the hours of stimulating discussions with excellent teachers and lively companions with whom I exchanged ideas while working at the universities of the United States. Among them were: Federico de Onís, Tomás Navarro Tomás, and Ángel del Río of Columbia University; Juan A. Centeno of Middlebury College; and the poets Pedro Salinas of Johns Hopkins University and Jorge Guillén of Wellesley College. These scholars lend the finest esthetic quality to Hispanic studies in North America, since their work combines learning with interpretive refinements. I owe many a profitable suggestion to these good friends and teachers.

The history of Hispanic American culture is still unwritten in its entirety and complexity and with that subtle and poetic intuition which any appraisal requires if it is to be more than a mass of chronologically coördinated data. Perhaps it is not too vain on my part to claim a modest role as a worker in this field of study. I am well aware that many topics are merely touched upon in the following pages, and that they call for more extensive treatment. I know too that any one of the questions raised—such as the pedagogy of the missionary effort, the fusion of Spanish and Indian elements to produce a *mestizo* art, the insulation and isolation of the baroque period, the rise of the insurgent attitude toward Spain in the latter half of the eighteenth century—can easily be subjects of separate monographs, each one bulkier than the whole of this synthesis. But if anything is as necessary as scholarly research, it is the perspective that we still lack on our inner history. This is much more difficult to deal with than the military feats and biographies that constitute so much of the historical writing of Hispanic America. Many aspects, moreover, call for revision and a change of methods. Today we cannot look at our historical evolution with the prejudices and limitations of nineteenth-century historians. Problems that they did not consider, or did not emphasize, now take on for us marked importance. And since time has cooled the hatreds and suspicions of earlier historians, it is now the moment to attempt, not the impossible ideal of an absolutely objective account, but one that at least may serve our aspirations and offer better answers to today's question marks. People in the twenty-first century will emphasize matters that escape our attention, and so the past is continually remade to satisfy the perennial and ever-changing demands of successive generations.

The Hispanic American historical writing that grew from the wars for independence, and to a large degree still continues, could never rise above current prejudices. In the first place, earlier writers labored under the illusion that history really began with them, and that when the colonies, newly freed from Spain, were called the "Republic of Venezuela," the "Republic of Peru," or the "Republic of Chile," something so novel was thereby engendered that all that had happened earlier could only be described by leaping a deep crevice that made any continuity virtually impossible. History took on the hue of the common political passions of the time. Romantic liberals erected a wall of contempt for, and negation of, the colonial period. By contrast, equally confused conservatives—even some of genuine talent like Lucas Alamán in Mexico—were convinced that all evil had come with the republic, and they yearned for the aristocratic social order of the former viceroys. Neither side was able nor wished to recognize that, above and beyond political forms and nomenclature, the same political forces were still operating and evolving, namely, the effects of the tremendous impact of the white conquerors on the indigenous peoples. As these pages may perhaps make clear, from the moment that the Europeans set foot in the New World, there began an unending conflict within the naturalized forms of civilized life. This difficulty arose from the complex and foreign ways of an imposed culture favoring privileged minorities that were relatively indifferent to the reality of their surroundings, and from the accumulation of unresolved problems originating in the Indian and hybrid masses. On observing such a vertical contrast in the struggling societies and nations of Spanish America, still un-identified as such, Alexander von Humboldt, in his admirable and still vital book on New Spain, was moved to reflect on the curious resemblance of that colonial world—both an El Dorado and a land of poverty, an area of rich silver and gold mines and of barefoot multitudes—to the contemporary Russian empire, where the refine-ment of the tsarist court and the small Europeanized groups clashed with the semibarbarism of the masses. Thus—although it may seem odd—there is a modern interest and validity in the pedagogical efforts of the sixteenth-century Pedro de Gante or Vasco de Quiroga to redeem the native Indian, not by burdening him with European learning, but rather by perfecting him in the arts and crafts that were a part of his age-old tradition. To reconcile an essentially manual culture with one of book learning and universities still re-mains the biggest educational problem in Spanish America.

After independence and the break-up of the former colonies into territorial compartments, a prematurely strong nationalism devel-oped, with each country thinking itself quite unlike its neighbor. Each fragment of the former empire forgot that what was essential for the later policy of our Indo-Spanish world was the original spirit-ual unity that the genius and prophetic vision of Simón Bolívar strove to organize into a vigilant force against the selfishness of pri-vate interests and of regional *caudillos* or strongmen. In spite of en-vironmental differences and contrasts, Spanish American reactions to the world since colonial days have a greater identity and family relationship than is generally realized. When the story of our coun-tries is presented as merely an addition to local histories, and so with a consequent loss of perspective, it becomes a repetition or parallel of identical phenomena. The intellectual and spiritual movements reaching us from Europe—Encyclopedism, liberalism, romanticism, and the like—were transformed. In like manner they affected the common denominators of a culture and historical spirit that had steadily solidified during three colonial centuries and that even now, taken as a whole, clearly distinguish, one from the other, the separate regions of the Western Hemisphere occupied by peoples of Hispanic and of Anglo-Saxon origins. The Spanish language is the greatest and truest instrument of identification of the inhabitants from the desert margins of the Rio Grande to the cold plains of Patagonia. Against nature's obstacles language and history present a feeling of brotherhood that, taking precedence over any future political or economic groupings, offers the best hope to the Hispanic American world and the guarantee of greatest promise. It devolves upon writers and thinkers of our countries constantly to strengthen the foundations of this understanding and to develop the rationale that may lift to a plane of true consciousness in the minds of our people what until now has been a mere emotion or a vital but unorganized instinct. May this book and possible sequels on so timely a subject be my modest tribute as a writer to so noble an idea!

MARIANO PICÓN-SALAS

New York, Columbia University,
January, 1944.

Contents

The Indian Legacy

AN ARCHAEOLOGICAL SUMMARY

In trying to answer the question of our earliest beginnings, those of us who are laymen in archaeology can only draw some tentative conclusions from the complicated debates of professional archaeologists to meet our need to conjure out of the dark night of prehistory an image and a concept of the nature of the first men and their activities in America. From the geological and anthropological point of view America truly deserves the designation "New World" (*Orbe Novo*) that Pietro Martire d'Anghera bestowed upon it in his elegant, humanistic Latin when he reported the surprising discovery to the enlightened Renaissance world. It was probably between 40,000 and 15,000 years ago (which, in geological time, was only yesterday) that fishermen or hunters of a Mongolian type whose features persist in American aborigines in spite of local differences, crossed over the natural bridge of the Bering Strait, either in a single wave or in successive ones, and started on their long wanderings about the Western Hemisphere in quest of more hospitable lands. These first invaders were men of the Stone Age, and their cultural achievements were probably limited to the use of fire, the crude flint ax, the bow and arrow, and possibly the beginnings of a rudimentary basketry. This hypothesis, however, does not exclude one put forth by French anthropologists to the effect that at some far distant time primitive navigators from Melanesia and Polynesia also may have reached the shores of Peru or Ecuador.

Vestiges of ancient cultures showing early stages of agriculture, pottery, and the oldest types of small carved figures have been found, mostly on the Mexican plateau—especially at Cuicuilco near Coyoacán, whose ruins are about five thousand years old, according to an estimate of the North American archaeologist Byron Cummings. These highlands of Mexico (Teotihuacán, Tenochtitlán, Cholula, Mitla, Monte Albán), like the Andean region of Peru, Ecuador, and Bolivia, were the early seats of intermediate cultures that, in the course of long centuries, evolved into higher forms of civilization. The peoples of the ancient culture on the Mexican plateau had already domesticated the most typical cereal of America—maize, or corn—whose sacred origin and vast benefit to mankind are recurring themes in all aboriginal mythology. Where was this extraordinary agricultural conquest first won? Archaeologists still dispute the matter. Some believe that the probable progenitor of our American staff of life was the wild *teocintle* of Mexico. There is speculation as to whether the early *euchlaena* was developed into edible maize on the high plain of Anahuac or whether its place of origin should be sought on the warm and humid gulf coast. Fossilized ears of maize have been found in ancient tombs of Peru. The Peabody Museum in Boston has so many specimens of primitive maize (North American, Peruvian, and Mexican) that it is almost impossible to come to a definite conclusion. It is certainly clear that the aborigines themselves associated their entrance into history with the fortunate discovery of this life-giving cereal. According to a legend about the nature of the world found in *Popol Vuh*, a sacred book of the Maya, the first men were made of maize. By shelling and grinding it until it fermented, the Ixmucané brewed nine beverages containing the substance that gave energy and strength to the human species. In the Aztec religion the beneficent Quetzalcóatl was represented as the discoverer of maize, the cult of which was symbolized by two other gods: the elegant and spirited Cinteotl and the goddess Xilonen, to whom a slave girl was sacrificed annually so that the maize would put forth the tenderest ears. Even today in Catholic festivals and at the celebration of the Corpus Christi the highland Indians of Peru and Bolivia empty pitchers of fermented *chicha* in homage to Pachacamac rather than to the Christian deity. The raw *muday*, a maize liquor well laced with saliva, is the standard beverage of hospitality among the Araucanian Indians of southern Chile.

The domestication of maize and the birth of the ceramic art, which is associated with agricultural activity, correspond to the "ancient cultural wave or waves" that have left their mark, all the way from Mexico to the Pacific coast of South America, on the food habits of the natives and on the primitive manufacture of small idols, containers for liquids, and *metates* to grind maize. Perhaps these or later contacts between the two continental areas explain some stylistic similarities in works of art noted both north and south. It can only surprise the layman in archaeology that at a much later date certain stylized variations of the jaguar found in the Chavín art of the Peruvian valley of Chicama curiously resemble the sculptures at Teotihuacán. The archaeologist Joyce believes that he found a strange confluence of the motifs of the two Americas in the aboriginal art of Nicaragua and Costa Rica. The large arc formed by the early cultures of the Antilles, Brazil, and the Venezuelan forests and plains was excluded from this apparent north-south movement, which seemed to be linked with the distant Guaraní family, by incursions of Caribs and Arauca Indians. It was only a few years ago that systematic archaeological research in our part of the hemisphere began to be organized, so that enigmas, wide gaps in knowledge, and vast unexplored areas render impossible any synthesis of the whole. Geography may explain why the Pacific slope of Central and South America still offers much richer and more impressive relics of the past than the Atlantic side, and also why the ancient cultures evolved grander styles in the salubrious surroundings of the lofty Andean plateaus. The moist east winds from the Atlantic caused the growth of a dense jungle on the tropic shores, whereas on the Pacific side the traveler goes from an arid and semidesert vegetation to the high coastal terrain sheltered by the Andes. The cold Humboldt Current is a different factor in South America: its effects are felt as far north as the southern shores of Ecuador, favorably modifying atmospheric conditions in that latitude and determining the special nature of the climate along the coast of Peru.

The "wave or waves of ancient culture," which modified and developed different peculiarities on coming in contact with varied environmental factors, must have originated a series of regional adaptations that progressively evolved into more complicated forms of political organization. Toward the end of the seventh century B.C., according to the calculations of the archaeologist Spingard, the Maya had already invented their calendar and had moved on from their early settlement in the Huasteca region north of Veracruz to the vicinity of Petén in Guatemala. But the first great states in either North or South America were probably formed during the fifteen centuries from A.D. 100 to the arrival of the Spaniards. The first Maya empire, which until the eighth century of the Christian era was situated in the Petén region of central Guatemala, in adjacent lands of Honduras, and on the Belice coast, went into a period of decline after that time. The beginnings of the new empire must be looked for about the tenth century in the more arid district of northern Yucatán. From the thirteenth century this empire came in violent contact with the cruder cultures of the Mexican Highlands—first the Toltec and later the Aztec—and by the fifteenth century the disintegration of the grandeur that was the Maya civilization was complete.

The conflicts between peaceful, sedentary populations and nomadic peoples from a harsher climate and with a stronger power drive largely explains the succession of nations and empires, as it does in the ancient history of the East. Thus it was that the stern military rigor of the Aztec supplanted the contemplative, poetic world of the Maya with its wealth of imaginative art and literature. In the aboriginal mythologies, as we shall presently see, the forces that may be termed the sustainers of life and the creators of culture are locked in eternal combat with the forces of destruction. In the Mexican world it is the symbolic struggle between Quetzalcóatl, a beneficent hero who teaches mankind the arts of agriculture and the crafts of artisans, and Tezcatlipoca, the god of night arrayed in a tiger skin who protects the wizards and the wicked. To wrest from the latter the control of the universe, Quetzalcóatl must himself don a tiger skin and rend Tezcatlipoca with his claws in a surprise attack. But that does not end the struggle, because Tezcatlipoca will attack in turn. Human history thus becomes a ceaseless battle; to appease the wrath of the gods, Quetzalcóatl, after descending into the realm of the dead, anoints the bones of all the departed generations with his sacrificial blood so that more peace-loving mortals may be born.

At the time of the first Maya empire two contrasting civilizations were flourishing in Peru. On the shores of Lake Titicaca and its lofty hinterland was the strange, abstract Tiahuanaco culture, whose geometric patterns, cold rigidity, lean monolithic representations of the human figure, and absence of feeling have suggested a connection with the mysterious, oceanic art of Easter island. The other was the coastal culture of the First Chimu and the First Nasca. In sharp contrast they depicted on their beautiful vases, with a polychromatic and dynamic realism, hunting and fishing scenes, ceremonial dances, and bedecked warriors going forth to battle. It is the most consummate art of portraiture in any aboriginal culture with its stylized abundance of fauna—including cats, jaguars, serpents, scorpions— together with an extraordinary inventiveness of decorative designs that, by kaleidoscopic changes and variations, express both a fertile imagination and an inner torment. If Tiahuanaco art is typical of the Andean highlands, whose stark landscapes invite abstraction and large-scale forms, the art of the coast is full of the light and brilliant colors of the tropics. The feeling for form and the striking beauty of the vases—on which the artists were so obsessed by their subject matter that they left no part of the surface undecorated—did not, however, exclude such disquieting elements as a throng of weird figures and diminutive monsters now and then found in the designs of their textiles and pottery. These included cats transformed into demons, demons shaped like birds, jaguars reminiscent of the Mexican ones at Teotihuacán, many-headed gods, and deified scorpions or centipedes. With its commingling of forms, fantastic arabesques, and marked independence of coloring, a very strange vase in the Gaffron de Schachtensee Collection resembles the boldest kind of present-day surrealism. In its center a monsterlike beast—possibly a puma—whose paws are being gnawed by stylized scorpions and from whose tail another head is emerging, offers a fascinating similarity to the weird, animal-like figures in Picasso's painting *Guérnica*.

Between the eighth and ninth centuries the Tiahuanaco culture descended from its Andean solitude to the Peruvian coast and gave rise to a curious and not completely harmonious fusion of highland symbolism and the coloring of coastal art. This style, extending possibly as far as the Manabí culture in Ecuador, had adorned the stone monuments of Hatuncolla on Lake Titicaca with some of the motifs of the hot lowlands, such as the iguana and the alligator, but was already showing signs of decline when the second Maya empire was developing in the eleventh and twelfth centuries. A reappearance of the old Chimu and Nasca cultures on the Peruvian coast coincided with the emergence of the earliest Inca culture in the highlands.

From the fourteenth to the sixteenth century the "empires," which the Spaniards were to destroy, were shaping up in both Mexico and Peru. We may refer to them as empires even though the social organization of the Aztec never achieved the centralization that the Inca did but more closely resembled a series of feudal baronies. Much less important in pre-Hispanic America at this time were the petty Chibcha kingdoms at Bogotá, Tunja, Guatabita, and Iraca which, if the Spanish Conquest had not occurred, might well have gravitated into the orbit of the Inca, whose influence already extended as far north as Popayán in Colombia. Possibly the Spaniards interrupted at an early stage an evolutionary trend toward large indigenous states and nationlike entities such as the Inca had almost attained in their empire and was barely suggested in the political organization of the Aztec.

For continued progress, however, these aboriginal civilizations had many technological handicaps. They lacked the horse and other domestic animals to lighten their labor; the wheel was unknown; and they had no real knowledge of metallurgy. If the religious and plastic arts of the Maya, Toltec, and Inca could compete with Oriental creations, in other respects they still had not progressed much beyond Neolithic man.

An unvarying lament against a world of grief and against the tragic surprise of existence was inextricably blended in the Indian symbols and in the profound sadness of their myths and songs. Life was forever in flux. The gods, pitiless in Aztec theology but good-natured and playful—even making conundrums—in Maya cosmology, were continually altering and changing the world. Against the things of the earth mankind had far fewer defenses. Such North American scholars as Spinden, Morley, and particularly Ellsworth Huntington have tried to prove that the collapse of the first Maya empire was the result of a drastic change of climate that made their habitat dank and overgrown, spread diseases—possibly epidemics of malaria—and thus weakened the inhabitants or forced them to look for more healthful surroundings.

Nature, which moved the Indians to symbolize their conceptions of the world in terrifying divinities, filled their lives—which had so few technological resources—with uncertainty and an immediate, oppressive sense of tragedy and disaster.

THE ABORIGINAL MIND

That not only the Maya but other peoples of America had a form of writing is a matter upon which recent archaeological investigations are now throwing light. The distinguished Mexican archaeologist Alfonso Caso has discerned in mural frescos at Teotihuacán a kind of writing in numerical dots and dashes which evidently substitutes an ideographic language for mere picture writing. The key to deciphering these ideograms is, however, still missing. Moreover, as Caso points out, writing or painting in these ancient cultures was a task of the instructed few. Among the Aztec, for example, it was a ritual open only to priests and the military who had undergone the rigorous and secret discipline of the *Calmecac*, a kind of advanced military and religious institute serving the ruling caste. To bring a few impressions of that vanished world to our modern consciousness we shall have to be content with inspecting a few old manuscripts—almost all written after the Spanish Conquest—in which the mythical story of a people is depicted amid a clutter of symbols and hieroglyphics on deerskin or *maguey* paper; or with the mural frescoes of temples, scenes painted on vases, and the written testimony gathered by the early chroniclers Sahagún, Motolinía, and Durán in Mexico and Poma de Ayala in Peru; or with the narratives of mythology such as the *Popol Vuh* or the *Book of Chilam Balam de Chumayel* which were written by Indian or half-caste scribes but betray European influences.

What does the aboriginal mind tell us? Although there are native differences as remarkable as those separating the Aztec from the distant world of the Inca—the blood-drunk fierceness of the former, for example, in contrast to the peaceful, orderly collectivism of the latter —the modern observer, even at this distance in time, can distinguish a subtle Indian atmosphere, an intangible something that profoundly divides the psychology and forms of ideation of the aborigine from those of his conqueror. By reading the poems that have come to us through the Spanish friars, and by interpreting the myths, I shall endeavor as far as possible to indicate in broad outline the native sensibility.

First and foremost, the Indian peoples conceived history as destiny and catastrophe, in marked contrast to the dynamic optimism of the Renaissance which the Spanish conquistador embodied in his own fashion. No concept was farther from the Indian mentality than the Western idea of progress. According to the awesome legend of the suns in Aztec theogony the universe has already been destroyed four times: by tigers, winds, showers of fire, and water. Each successive destruction has engendered a new race of men that inherits nothing from its predecessor and is equally helpless in the face of destiny. The crude giants that fed on wild acorns perished along with the first sun; they were the useless and foolish inventions of the god Tezcatlipoca. The people surviving the destruction of the second world by hurricanes were changed into monkeys as an example of the willfulness of the gods. To create a new sun after the end of the fourth world, the lords of heaven, assembled at Teotihuacán, were obliged to institute the first sacrifices. Two of the gods—the valiant poor deity and the timid rich one—were consumed in a vast bonfire; from the ashes of one emerged the new sun, and from the ashes of the other the moon. "Essential to the Aztec religion," writes Alfonso Caso, "is human sacrifice, for if men could not exist without the creation of gods, the latter in turn must be supported by sacrificial offerings of the magic substance, the vital essence contained in the human blood and heart." In Aztec theogony even life in heaven was continual warfare and sacrifice. For the sun to shine each morning, Huitzilopochtli—the fierce young god who, in the course of each day, journeys from the dwelling place of the living to the chill domain of the dead—must eternally engage in renewed battle with the stars and the moon. He is helped in this daily strife—symbolized by the fiery serpent—by the souls of the warriors who have died in the *guerras floridas* or on the sacrificial stone. To be reborn the next day, however, he must be gathered into the belly of the earth mother at sunset. But all this cosmic struggle would be inadequate if mankind did not give the sun the *chalchiuatl*—warm human blood, the beverage that nurtures divinity best and enables it to confront so many perils with energy. Nourished by the red liquor of sacrifice, the sun boldly faces the squadrons of warriors—the southern stars—which seek to block his path across the sky.

The idea of immolation indicates how life forever feeds upon death. Coatlicue—the mother goddess who symbolizes the earth and into the womb of whom the sun sinks each evening so as to be born again the next day—is also called the "devourer of offal" because she feeds upon human cadavers. Her feet and hands are claws with which she grasps death and putrescence in order to beget life anew. In Maya mythology this essential pessimism is no less somberly expressed. When the builder and the maker spirits decide to destroy by flood one of the many worlds they have created, and when Digger of Faces, Death Bat, Wizard Turkey, and Wizard Owl come to finish off mankind, the drama of the universe occurs with the same unexpectedness and the same merciless terror. In the *Popol Vuh*, "Men try to climb into their abodes, but their collapsing abodes make them fall. They try to climb trees, but the trees cast them far off. They try to crawl into holes, but the holes scornfully reject their faces." The account ends: "Such was the destruction of a people fated to be destroyed, fated to be annihilated. Their mouths, their faces, all were destroyed, all were annihilated." Another mythical tale in the *Popol Vuh*, explaining the preordained circle in which life revolves, tells the story of the animals that went to carry a message to the gallant young ballplayers who had not returned from the country of Xibalba, the land of death. The first creature to start was a louse. On the way the louse meets a toad, which devours the louse. The toad takes up its journey until it meets a viper. The viper eats the toad, and a hawk eats the viper. Thus a fateful chain continues until the last creature falls before the unerring blowgun of the gods.

Now and then in Aztec lyric poetry, in spite of a ritualistic formalism and unapprehended symbols that erect barriers to our ways of thinking and feeling, the theme of total disillusionment and the fragility of life emerges—although its sources are quite different from those inspiring the lyric verse of western Europe. In the anthology compiled by the Mexican humanist Garibay, there is a most curious "Song of Sadness," the two basic ideas of which—life's journey to death, and life as a mere deceptive dream—remind us immediately of the famous *Couplets* of the Spanish poet Jorge Manrique and of Calderón's celebrated play *Life's a Dream*. The anonymous author of the "Song of Sadness" wrote:

I weep and am distressed when I remember
that we shall leave behind the lovely flowers, the lovely songs;
. . . not a second time will they be conceived,
not a second time will they be born.

And now they are about to depart from the earth . . .
. . . Oh, where will this heart of mine dwell?
Where will be my home? Where my lasting abode?
Ah, I am shelterless on earth . . .

. . . But what truth can I utter here,
Oh, Thou through whom all things exist?
We but dream, like one who tumbles half asleep from bed:
I speak only of things earthly, for no one can speak aught else.

. . . Though precious stones and soft ointments be offered,
no one, oh Thou through whom all things exist,
no one of us on earth can say aught of worth.

But perhaps this very feeling of inexorable fate gave the native cultures their stoicism and their indifference to pain, for both the Aztec
and the Inca—though for differing social and political ends—trained
their people in such mute, ascetic calisthenics. Among the Inca the
well-ordered, collectivist society lent itself to such institutions as the
mitimaes, which permitted, at the mere whim of the state, the transfer of families and whole villages far from their native region. Among
the Aztec this stoicism led to the support of such a cruel caste as the
Knight Eagles and Tigers, who as servants of the sun were charged
with providing food for the sun and waging *la guerra florida*. The
impressive Aztec sculpture called the "Knight Eagle," which at first
view calls to mind a twelfth-century European Crusader, embodies
the native ideal of a stern, rigidly controlled fortitude. Reserve, restraint, a wrapt absorption in duty—these are the qualities that this
block of andesite, which registers neither wrath nor the faintest glim-
mer of a smile, seems to communicate to us. The terrible discipline
of *Calmecac*—a kind of institute for nobles that subjected them to
severe fasting and purification exercises to overcome sleep and cold
—shaped the ruling caste.

The stoic acceptance of suffering and the exalted impassiveness of
the Indian in the face of torture and death were to be the earliest
themes of Spanish American epics. Some of these stoic heroes were:
The Mexican Cuauhtémoc; Sorocaima and Guaicaipuro of Venezuela; and Caupolicán, Lautaro, and Rengo, the great chieftains of
Ercilla's poem *La Araucana*. Aztec mythology promised the gallant
warrior who died in battle the most beautiful transformation: to be
changed into a hummingbird, the delicate, glittering bird that feeds
on flowers.

There is no inconsistency between this stoicism and two other
traits apparently general in the aboriginal world: humility and melancholy. In the *Popol Vuh*, for instance, the older brothers of the Mas-

ter Wizard Magician, who were "very great musicians, singers, and all-knowing wisemen," were punished by the gods because they had humiliated their younger companions. They climbed a tree to catch birds, but the tree grew so fast that they could not get down. Each tried to remove his loincloth to use as a rope, but it changed into a tail and each brother turned into a monkey. Earlier the offended Wizard Magician and his younger brothers had said: "In their hearts they have debased us to the level of servants; we shall humble them accordingly." The sadness of the Indian—so well interpreted by the Inca Garcilaso de la Vega in his sensitively written *Royal Commentaries of the Inca*—is one of the psychological traits of the natives that impressed the Spaniards from the outset. About Aztec songs Friar Diego Durán wrote in the sixteenth century: "They were so plaintive that the mere sound and the dance brought a feeling of sadness. I have seen dancing accompanied by lovely songs that were sometimes so plaintive that it filled me with sorrow and I listened with a heavy heart." Commenting on a native dance surviving in the Jauja region of Peru, a modern historian—José de la Riva Agüero—wrote about the Quechua Indians: "Theirs is tender, gentle, doleful poetry of naïve charm and pastoral softness, suddenly darkened by fits of the most tragic despair. More reserved and bound by tradition than any other people, this race possesses the gift of tears and the cult of memory. Guardians of mysterious tombs and forever mourning among these cyclopean ruins, their favorite diversion and bitter consolation are to sing about the woes of their history and the poignant grief that lies in their hearts. Near Juaja the Indian maidens, who represent the chorus of princesses in the popular pageant of the Inca, still intone the words as they bow with infinite piety before Huáscar, the vanquished monarch: 'Let us wipe away his tears and, to relieve his distress, let us take him to the country where he may breathe the fragrance of the flowers—*Huaytaninta musquichipahuay.*'"

The whole outlook of the native is both symbolic and poetic. Against the logic, realism, and the anthropocentric sense of European culture, the Indian rears his world of mysterious relationships. What makes the pre-Hispanic monumental art so alien and incomprehensible to us (aside from a mere appraisal of its forms) are precisely those symbols whose key is lost to us and whose religious and philosophical subtleties can be interpreted only by a small circle of initiates. A complex system of associated ideas, which combine in limited permutations, depict the concepts and strange mental images on the countenances of the gods. Tlaloc, for example, is the god of water, vegetation, and lightning, but the variety of atmospheric phenomena associated with rain—hail, ice, floods, soft white or stormy clouds, bountiful harvests or droughts—must all be expressed by the hideous mask of the divinity. The features of the face are formed by the intertwining of two serpents, which, after twisting in a sinuous arabesque, join their fangs over the mouth of the god. The mask is painted blue—the color of water and the clouds. Another part of the body is painted black to represent the storm-laden clouds. Rising above the fearful head is a quetzal feather symbolizing the luxuriant tassel of maize that the rain has watered.

The "masked word" (*nahuatlotolli*) was the means—incomprehensible to the uninitiated—by which the priest and wizard conjured up mysterious forces. In the Maya *Book of Chilam Balam*, Kaat Naat—the "lord who questions"—speaks to men, surprising and confusing them by his figurative language. He will ask them, for example, to satisfy his hunger by fetching the trunk of the ceiba tree, the three twisted things, and the live rattan vine. The trunk of the ceiba tree is a lizard, the three twisted things are an iguana's tail, and the live rattan vine is a pig's intestines. Spanish customs and Catholic rites had already profoundly influenced the Maya people when Juan José Hoil—or whoever it was—wrote the *Book of Chilam Balam*, but these innovations undergo the same sort of symbolic transformation. Among many other enigmas the Lord Questioner demands that the sun be brought to him on a plate and that the great green tiger must be seated on the sun drinking its blood. Since he is not understood, he explains this hieroglyph by saying that the sun is a "sacred fried egg" and that "the green tiger squatting on it and drinking its blood is green chili which contains tiger essence." The blessing the Catholic parish priest bestows upon his Indian flock at the end of the Mass is the "lance of heaven thrust into the heart's core."

The esoteric character of native poetry moved Father Durán to re-
mark in the sixteenth century: "All their poems are composed of
such obscure metaphors that scarcely anyone can understand them
if he does not deliberately study and discuss them to ascertain their
true meaning." Yet the purest vein of poetry is struck in their complex symbolism. The ornamental elements recurring most frequently
in Aztec lyric verse are flowers, birds, and delicate stones. With a certain quaint ingenuousness Father Durán has related the wonder-
ment stirred in him by a dance in honor of Huitzilpochtli when he
witnessed it for the first time: "They performed it crowned with
roses and with bowers of these blossoms all about the *momoztli*
of the temple of their great god Huitzilpochtli. They made a house
of roses and also trees by hand full of sweet-smelling flowers, under
which they seated the goddess Xochiquetzalli. As they danced young
lads descended, some dressed like birds and others like butterflies,
all beautifully arrayed in luxuriant green, blue, scarlet, and yellow
plumes. Then they climbed into the trees, passing from limb to limb,
sipping the dew on the roses. At this juncture the gods appeared, the
Indians representing them bedecked in the same fashion as the divinities on the altars. With long blowguns in hand they kept shoot-
ing at imaginary birds flitting through the trees, from out of which
the goddess Xochiquetzalli came to meet them. Taking their hands
she had them sit beside her, thus bestowing the homage and dignity
that they had merited from the gods." Out of the heart of the flowers, as a short Aztec poem reads, comes the melodious song that the
poet pours forth. The blue flower and the red flower were presented
to the young prince and the victorious warrior; yellow flowers "perfume the realm of death." In another poem, life is compared to a
web-footed, fire-colored bird that wings off into the heart of the plain
in the kingdom of death.

A more intimate, modest, and tender note, perhaps, is struck in
the lyrics of the Inca which Ventura García Calderón calls "poetry
of the dawn, full of starry constellations, cotton flakes, and gentle
doves." It is the mournful *yaraví* or the domestic *haraví*. What the
glittering hummingbird and the precious stones are to Mexican
poetry, so to the Quechua world is the gentle llama—the companion

and helpmate of the Indian—or the crystalline waterfall in the mountain which the Inca knew how to control and care for as have no other people. The lyric animism of the Inca, whose religion had freed itself of the cosmic terror of the Aztec, invented myths of such gentle poetry as, for example, the one about the weary stone that, on rolling down from the lofty heights of the Andes to help build one of the sovereign's forts, became exhausted in dropping over precipices and by mankind's treatment; hollowed in it were eye sockets with which to weep tears of blood. The rain theme is not set forth in so frightening a myth as the Mexican one about Tlalco, but rather in the story of the maiden whose pitcher of life-giving water is shattered over the world when her youthful and impetuous brother, the lightning, comes to destroy it by his violence; but on other occasions she manages to save her pitcher and over mankind she pours its mild torrent of gentle water to ripen the seeds in the ground. In contrast to the warlike frenzy of the Aztec, the Quechua persistently sang of peace. In the prayers to Huiracocha, collected by Cristóbal de Molina in his *Account of the Fables and Religious Rites of the Inca*, the god is asked "to increase the population that the people and the land may be free of peril," that "men may live in health and wisdom with their children and descendants, walking in the paths of righteousness and without thoughts of evil," and that since men must eat and drink, "may their food, the fruits of the land, and the potatoes become more bountiful so that they may not suffer hunger or hardship but that they may grow and thrive." And the people pray that there be "no ice or hail," that "people may live long and not perish in their youth," and that they "may eat and live in peace." The ideal of the paternalistic state is set forth in a short prayer to the goddess of the earth: "Oh, Earth Mother, keep thy son the Inca upon thyself in peace and quiet. *Pachamcama casillacta quispillacta capac ynca huahuay quicla marcari atalli.*" The pessimism of the Quechua, gentler and more veiled than that of the Aztec, perceives a symbol of sorrow and the fate of man in the *pukuy-pukuy*, a small bird of the hills, hatched in the loneliest nest, which darts about the gorges and peaks of the Andes "seeing the straw and the whistling wind." An obsession of unshed tears—a sobbing that does not quite dare break out—haunts every *yaraví*. The dew of the night "is the tears of the moon." Weeping is the "juice of grief." "*Unoy uniquellam apariuan*," "the tears are drowning me," chants the chorus of youths in one of the collective songs that Huaman Poma de Ayala recorded in the sixteenth century. As a social attitude this pessimism breeds mistrust. "Whenever thou seest a stranger crying over thy sorrow, inside he is laughing. Take care of thine own herd . . . ," admonishes a contemporary Quechua song of the Cajamarca region.

Such tribes as the Araucanians of Chile, the Caribs of Venezuela, and the Apalaches of Florida—hardly at an intermediate level of culture in the sixteenth century—waged the most savage warfare against the Spanish conquistador. The Indian of Mexico and of Peru, who had lost his empire, seemed to fall back into the melancholy, the shadowy nostalgia that was destined to have its finest esthetic expression in the prose chronicle *The Royal Commentaries of the Inca* by the Inca Garcilaso de la Vega. Long before the first great uprisings in the eighteenth century the Indians and half castes, who had learned the language of the conquistador—among them Alva Ixlilxochitl, Alvarado Tezozomoc, and Huamán de Ayala— would write chronicles and elegies of the past glory of their race. The Indian Juan José Hoil, or whoever wrote the splendid Maya work *The Book of Chilam Balam* in the eighteenth century, turned to the legendary fatalism of his people and to the chronology of the *katunes*, who had engendered and transformed so many different species of humanity, to explain and bewail the disaster that had overwhelmed his race. *The Book of Chilam Balam* says that "from the east they came, and when they arrived they said that they made their first meal of custard apples." For this reason they were called the "foreign eaters of custard apples." Consoling himself by imagining a new *katun* through whom the Indian race might rise once more, the author writes in the florid and melancholy language of the Maya: "Every moon, every year, every day, every wind comes, and likewise passes away." In the deep crevasse of sorry defeat he can dream of a golden age, which every race puts at the beginning or at the end of their destiny: "When all men lived in health; when there was no illness, no aching bones, no smallpox, no fever in the chest, no pain in the stomach, no wasting away"; when "men walked erect and straight" before the "*dzules* [invaders] taught us fear, and before they hurt the plant and sucked the honey of the flowers of others so that their own blossoms might bloom."

The First Impact

II

Except in the dim past of Oriental history mankind has perhaps never known a conflict between peoples of such opposite ways of life as the Hispanic Conquest of America. It was a clash of races, economic attitudes, and contrasting modes of existence that still complicates the problems of social relationships in every country of Latin America. Anglo-Saxon civilization in North America was able to be far more flexible socially because it had only to confront the difficulty of populating vacant land after sweeping the unfortunate nomadic Indians from their vast plains and prairies, and also because, uninhibited by religious principles, it had adapted to its own use the economic ideas of the modern age. The capitalistic yeast was already working in the Puritan faith and spirit. From empty wilderness the Anglo-Saxon created his own community with a will like that of Robinson Crusoe and a resourcefulness that the Spaniard was unable to display in the relatively crowded world of strange inhabitants and highly developed rites and customs that he encountered at Tenochtitlán and at Cuzco. In North America democracy was able to thrive with the gradual rise of a people who considered themselves equals and had only to scale economic class barriers. In Hispanic America, on the contrary, the totally dissimilar cultures of the conquerors and the conquered and the semifeudal order established through the institution of the *encomienda* accentuated caste differences. There the democratic process could not evolve in an orderly manner as it did in the United States, but only through bloody upheavals beginning with Indian uprisings in the eighteenth century and continuing in the great battles of the wars of independence and the later fighting between *caudillos* in the nineteenth century. The almost constant civil strife in Hispanic America was not only for a better distribution of economic wealth, but it was also an expression of animosities of the "humbled" and the "angered." The genesis of these struggles, incidentally, can be traced back to the conflicts among the sixteenth-century conquerors of Peru and the opposition of the first settlers and holders of *encomiendas* to the so-called New Laws abolishing certain property rights which the Spanish viceroy and the Audiencia tried to enforce. Isn't the diabolic adventure of Lope de Aguirre, known to history as "Tyrant," against Peruvian authorities in the sixteenth century a kind of early epic of wrath and indignation? And isn't there an epic quality of muddled rebelliousness in his famous letter to Philip II with its indictment of the administration of the Indies by a court of common soldiers?

But before social stratification and the institutional apparatus have crystalized that resentment, let us consider the basic problems that arose in Hispanic America from the collision of different cultures. It is unfair to blame sixteenth-century Spaniards for a lack of anthropological insight or for a belief that only their own way of life had validity. It should be remembered, too, that every conquistador felt obliged by his religious convictions to further the spread of the Christian faith, which the Spaniard identified with his very being. To him this endeavor was the one thing that justified the violent quest for gold and the cruelty of war. The allegations of good intentions and the sophistry by which the conqueror eased his conscience make one of the strangest chapters in the moral history of the time. The last will and testament of Hernán Cortés offers an example. Fearing the imminence of death, and aware of the theological and juridical preoccupations of his age ("whether war against the Indians was a just war," "whether Indians can be enslaved on the pretext of teaching them the true faith"), the conqueror of Mexico felt that his sins required expiation and absolution. Since the outcome of the theological debate on the justice or injustice of wars of conquest was still undecided, Cortés said: "Since there has been and still remains much doubt and difference of opinion about whether the natives of New Spain taken as prisoners of war or by exchange can be enslaved lawfully and in good conscience and, since the matter is still unsettled, I direct that everything possible be ascertained regarding what should be done to discharge one's conscience in this connection . . . I charge and direct Martín Cortés, my son and successor and all his heirs to my estate, to make every effort to learn what is appropriate to satisfy my conscience and theirs." How ingeniously the mind of those times tried to reconcile what seems irreconcilable in a Christian formula: the desire for riches and power and the propagation of the Christian faith!

To justify warring upon the Indians, Martín Fernández de Enciso, a geographer and member of Spanish expeditions turned theologian, drew a parallel from the Old Testament in the story of the Israelites contending with the idolaters over the Promised Land: "And then Joshua sent to demand of the people in the first city which was Jericho that they forsake and hand over that land to him, for it was his because God had given it to him." Illustrating the Spaniard's need to legalize his scruples by formal procedures a curious document was drawn up—"Requirement." It was a sort of outdoor theological treatise that every conquistador was obliged to read to possibly hostile natives before sounding his war trumpets, touching off his culverins, or charging his horses against the startled, bronze-hued tribes. Beginning with a long genealogy of the Christian faith, which starts with the first chapter of Genesis, this official paper passed on to the story of the Passion and death of Christ, explained the institution of the Papacy and Alexander VI's donation of that part of the world to the Catholic Monarchs of Spain. It then provided a proclamation and due notice that the conquistador must read in the shade of some tropic tree before making a military onslaught. The document then concluded with a statement that anticipates Don Quixote by at least a hundred years: "If you do not acknowledge this by promptly obeying the Pope and His Majesty the King of Castile, and becoming his vassals, or if you maliciously delay in doing so, I declare unto you that with God's help I shall advance upon you with fire and sword and I shall make war upon you everywhere and in every way I can."

Well known is the answer that the fierce Indians in the Sinú region of present-day Colombia gave to the intrepid interpreter who translated the Requirement to them in behalf of the conquistadors. The Indians quite agreed that "there was but one God" but, "so far as the Pope's saying that he was Lord of the Universe and that he had bestowed all this land upon the king of Spain, he must have been drunk when he did so, because he was giving away what he did not own. As for the king who asked for and accepted the gift, he must have been insane, because he was asking for what belonged to others. Let him come and get it, and they would display his head on the end of a pole like one of their enemies that they showed me exposed in the same fashion."

With the realism of a man well seasoned by the Conquest, Gonzalo Fernández de Oviedo commented that the Requirement, into which learned advocates of Castile had poured their best theology and juridical scruples, was sometimes read to the Indians "after lining them up with no translator or interpreter and without either the reader or the natives understanding what it was all about. Nor did they have an opportunity to reply to what was read, for they were immediately pushed along like prisoners, and laggards were beaten with clubs."

Even if one conquistador acted in good faith, his system of values and moral judgments was totally unlike that of the natives. This situation dramatically affected the debate on the capabilities of the Indians and the rights that would be granted them. The controversy began on the island of Santo Domingo after Father Montesinos had preached his first, fiery sermon against the Spanish planters and after Father Las Casas in Spain had denounced the incredible abuses suffered by the hapless natives. The Spaniard's idea of "capability" related, of course, entirely to the Hispanic way of life. No mind was yet able to view the Indian from within and to judge him by his natural responses and reactions, as men of the caliber of Sahagún— precursors of American anthropology—would go far toward doing several decades later. Soldiers and settlers, calloused by Indian wars, gave their testimony to the Jeronimite friars sent by Cardinal Cisneros, presumably acquiescing to the urgings of these clergymen to unburden their consciences by telling what they knew. Among these deponents were such men as Gonzalo de Ocampo, conqueror of Cumaná; Juan de Ampiés, governor of Coro; and the ill-fated Lucas Vázquez de Ayllón. A study of these materials, which Lewis Hanke has exhaustively made in his *The Spanish Struggle for Justice in the Conquest of America*, gives, as few other documents do, the clearest and most immediate impression of what Spaniards of different classes and occupations felt about the Indians. Many of these "repentant" individuals confess astonishment at the rude and primitive concept of economic value which could move the natives of the Antilles to exchange their best—and only—hammock for a small mirror, glass beads, or a pair of scissors. The primary and most exclusive measure of value was the desire for an object. The easygoing natives often felt inconvenienced by the clothing given them by the Spaniards as a special mark of favor. More than one Indian, when compelled to attend Mass in such close-fitting apparel, cast it off and went home as naked as Adam in the Garden of Eden. Penalties in the form of personal disgrace or dishonor occasionally imposed by the Spanish overlords to cure the natives of their "vices" had hardly any effect, nor did they receive any sanction from the tribe. Juan de Ampiés, who must have cut off many ears and flogged many Indians in the harsh conquest of the Coro region, complained with the air of a stern and disillusioned pedagogue that most of these punishments were quite useless because the poor devils never did learn thrift and honesty. Another Spanish overlord noted that when an Indian was made to work and given a good supply of food, he and his squaw would eat up a whole week's rations in a single day. Almost everyone agreed that it would be hard to teach the aborigines to work like Castilian farmers. The Spaniards bound the Indians from a roving, nomadic existence to a regime in which they must "pan gold, till plots of land, sell its products, and work for wages." This violent clash of cultures during the first years of colonization in the Antilles frequently caused the frightened natives to flee to the hills or to commit suicide. Those unable to endure the invader's coercion took their escape from life by drinking the juice of the bitter yucca plant. The habit of running away from their masters, first acquired by the Indians and later by the Negro slaves, quickly became a common occurrence in the early days of Hispanic America.

Although great differences in cultural evolution separated the Maya, Aztec, and Inca from the primitive islanders, the shock of contact with the white man was more pronounced in the ancient "empires" on the mainland. Besides the most refined and elemental practices exisiting side by side in the superior organization of those advanced societies the Spaniard had to contend, as the Peruvian archaeologist Valcárcel has observed, with other incongruities unprecedented in European experience: "There were contrasts in these cultural entities which involved curiously dissimilar elements. For example, the very same person who dressed in garments of the finest texture and in exquisite taste might wear a metallic disk or nose ornament suspended from a perforated septum, or he might carry around with him the shrunken head of an enemy as a trophy. And hand in hand went such opposite practices as converting a foe's skull into a drinking vessel or bestowing special privileges upon it if the deceased was a defeated leader who had acknowledged the supreme authority of the Inca emperor." Even in the accounts of their exploits that the conquistadors had written with an understandable proud bias, and before another kind of history revealed what the native thought, there are constant expressions of surprise, alarm, and wonder alternating with Spanish boastfulness and vainglory.

Bernal Díaz del Castillo, who often holds his nose in his wonderfully detailed story, tells of his disgust and nausea at the fearful and awful stench of the Aztec temples, the objects he saw for sale in the *tianguis* (markets), and certain sexual habits that were "much too Greek." Yet, at the same time he cannot help admiring the thoughtful consideration and restraint with which Moctezuma treated his women, which was in marked contrast to the crudity of the Spaniards brutalized by tropical wilds and years of warfare. The cleanliness and courtesy of the Aztec monarch appear as the very reverse of the rough ways and coarseness of his companions in arms. Looking back and reflecting on the Spanish Conquest from the melancholy eminence of his old age, Bernal Díaz—"aged and poor, with a daughter to marry off, with grown-up, bearded sons and still others to be raised," and now a worn-out veteran unable to journey to Madrid to present an account of his services rendered before His Majesty—tells how the Spaniards stopped the Indians "from making human sacrifices and committing obscene acts." Then he goes on to tell how the Audiencia of Mexico under Nuño de Guzmán had ordered "so many slaves branded" that it brought protests from even the most hardhearted.

If the frequent argument of the sixteenth-century Spanish overlords was the "sloth and indolence" of the Indians, it must be said that the war-toughened conquistador lost much of his own diligence and industrious habits after growing accustomed to cheap and submissive slave labor. Before being long in Mexico and Peru the hard fighters had fathered the sixteenth-century equivalents of playboys and wastrels. The generation that fought was succeeded by a generation that enjoyed the fruits of victory. And, according to Bernal Díaz, the first judges of the Audiencia were not only much given to "branding Indians but to attending more banquets than court sessions" and were "indulging in love affairs and rolling dice."

The Spanish soldier, unlike the Puritan settler, cheerfully cohabited with Indian women and—like Gonzalo Guerrero, of whom Bernal Díaz speaks, even preferred the "scarred face and pierced ear lobes" of the native female. From the very beginning, his sexual potency highlighted the psychic duality and fusion of blood and customs characterizing our cultural complex today. This explains why we have been unable to assume such obviously modern and practical ways as those of the United States. Ceremonies and rites peculiar to the Habsburg Spain of Charles V and of Moctezuma existed side by side or in hybrid form in many corners of Hispanic America. Remnants of a caste system still linger in many of our countries among a large part of our indigenous and rural population. The Spanish Conquest was not solely responsible for this condition which was already a part of the social organization of the Aztec and the Inca. The aim in several of our countries today is to enable the Indian to make use of the techniques and resources that his conqueror had mastered, or for the ruling class to solve the riddle that lies so deeply in the troubled eyes of the natives. This situation, in the minds of those who judge by European standards, is the cause of the apparent contradictions in our social process, and it explains why the civilizing effort of a Rivadavia in Argentina could be balked by the semibarbarous regression to the dictatorial rule of a Juan Manuel de Rosas. And it is this phenomenon that gave rise to the strange mystery of the nineteenth-century despot Francia of Paraguay, who so intrigued Carlyle. This is the opposite side of the Hispanic American coin— the side that is still dark passion rather than reason, that explodes in sudden, unexpected turbulence. Sometimes it is a bloody chieftain like Melgarejo of Bolivia or Pancho Villa of Mexico who has voiced the frustration and resentment of the masses better that the cultivated man of learning with his civilized methods.

The secret of our psyche is to be ferreted out more often in the indirect channel of emotions and esthetics than in a strictly logical causality which is artificial after all everywhere in history. It is enveloped in the semantic mystery of our Castilian speech of creoles, mulattoes, and Indians which absorbs new essences and manufactures new words; it is that imported Castilian with its "Americanisms" which has amalgamated the intimate expressions and metaphors of the aborigines and those of the Spaniard living in a completely different world. It is expressed in music, rites, festivals, and dances; it is evident in the work of the unknown laborer who, in the monuments of the colonial age, combined his own decorative idiom with the European style of his model. Thus it is that the synthesis of Spanish America is a hybrid mixture rather than being either a proud and haughty Hispanism on one hand or an indigenism seeking to return to its pre-Hispanic origins on the other.

Miscegenation in Latin America is far more than a mere mingling of blood and race; indeed, it is a bringing together in the temple of history of the dissident temperaments, dispositions, forms, and ways of life in which our antagonistic tendencies have developed. Not even in the most colorful pages of Herodotus, confined as they are to the narrow bounds of the classic world, could the story be told of such an ambitious human undertaking and of such a remarkable conjunction of dissimilar elements, nor could they offer that curious mingling of sudden fear and wonder that moved Bernal Díaz del Castillo to declare, on gazing down at Tenochtitlán: "It looked like the enchanted things related in the romance of chivalry, *Amadis of Gaul*."

The Spanish Conquest

III

THE TWO HISTORICAL THESES

From the historical point of view it now seems useless (though fruit-ful enough from an ethical standpoint) to reopen the debate—which began twenty years after Columbus landed in the Antilles—as to whether the Spanish Conquest was a Christian crusade or whether it was an irruption of violence and pillage, as Bartolomé de las Casas branded it. It does honor to the sixteenth-century Spanish mind that this controversy could arise even against "reasons of state," and it is interesting to compare the mental outlook of a Bartolomé de las Casas, who was still living on the borderland between the Middle Ages and the Renaissance, with that of a modern poet such as Kip-ling, the bard of British imperialism in India. Spain put forward the same arguments in the sixteenth-century dispute that the enemies of its colonial empire later used against it for political rather than re-ligious reasons. In the eighteenth century, similarly, the British were anxious to gain admittance of their trade and shipping to the latest overseas routes rigidly controlled by the monopolistic policies of the Castilian crown. In Las Casas's prose, rough but infused with warm feeling, there appears for the first time an idyllic vision of the native and his ways, an image of an innocent world turned into one of cruelty and avarice. It was, indeed, the same kind of summons be-fore the bar of justice that a Marmontel or an Abbot Raynal would formulate in the pre-Romantic mind of the eighteenth century.

This dispute—really insoluble because a large mass of evidence

27

can be adduced for either side—has, particularly since the nineteenth century, kept at odds two political currents of Spanish American historical thought: the colonial and traditionalist, emphasizing the predominance of Spanish elements in our culture, and the liberal and revolutionary, vehemently proclaiming its complete break with Spain. In defending the conquistadors against the inflamed homilies of Las Casas, the sixteenth-century historian López de Gómara sought to find positive values of creativity and civilization in the Conquest with which to temper the pessimism of that "Apostle of the Indians." Gómara said: "The Spaniards gave beasts of burden to relieve the natives of drudgery, wool to wear for modesty's sake if they liked rather than as a necessity, and meat to eat which they were without. The Spaniards showed them the use of iron and of oil lamps to improve their way of living; they gave them a system of money so that they would know how to buy and sell and what they had and owed. They taught them Latin and other subjects, which are worth a lot more than all the silver taken from them, because with literacy they become men whereas the silver was of little or no advantage to them. And so they were benefited by being conquered and, even more, by becoming Christians."

Gómara's thesis was revived in the nineteenth century by the renowned Mexican historian Lucas Alamán when he listed Spain's contributions to Spanish American life in minute detail. And he countered the often-drawn parallel between English colonization in the north and Spanish in the south by praising miscegenation and the cultural originality of the Spanish experiment which, unlike the English, deliberately sought to incorporate native elements. As the romantic period brought cultural nationalism into prominence, Alamán wrote with a certain naïve candor: "Writers in the United States must look abroad for subject matter. In the story of our past we find a wide field for poetry and history and for the study of antiquities by bringing the light of philosophy and criticism to them." In other words, whereas North American colonization was merely a shifting of Europe to new areas, Spanish American culture was a grafting of things Hispanic on an indigenous stock. To Alamán this meant that the destructive force of the Conquest was not so extreme as to wipe out every trace of original expression, and that what was destroyed was balanced by what was added.

In correcting the misapprehensions of English historical writing and propaganda, Alamán might also have emphasized still another merit of Spain that stands out in bold relief when compared with British colonial activities in the American tropics. If the British proved good colonizers in North America, southern Australia, and New Zealand, where a temperate climate made the transplanting of the mother country's pattern of living relatively easy, they were less successful in their tropical colonies. The traditions of European life, culture, and intellectual refinement that Spain left as its mark on Cuba and Puerto Rico were never equaled in the inferior trading-post kind of settlement that the English established at Jamaica in the very same area of the Caribbean. The Cuban writer Ramiro Guerra has made a well-documented study of this matter in his valuable book *Sugar and Population in the Antilles*. If the Spaniard permanently settled in our warmer regions and the resulting miscegenation created communities that eventually developed a nationalistic spirit, the Englishman preferred to keep aloof from other racial groups and have little to do with them other than as master and serf. Although sovereignty over Puerto Rico passed from Spain to the United States, even the most unobservant traveler will note a vigorous national spirit there that is hardly discernible in Jamaica. What is essentially local —resting on tradition, strong family ties, history, and a literature boasting of influential figures whose names are identified with its collective ideals and sentiments—keeps a regional consciousness alive. In tropical Jamaica—excellent producer of sugar cane and rum that it is—no De Hostos as in Puerto Rico and no José Rizal as in the Spanish Philippines have arisen as interpreters of an incipient nationalism. In Great Britain's tropical possessions, such as Jamaica and Trinidad, it is nearly impossible for groups as alien to each other as Africans, Hindus, or Asiatic coolies working under white bosses to have an awareness of a different historical consciousness. The Spanish colonies—nuclei of future republics—were true overseas provinces. Bringing hot lands under cultivation and carrying an urban culture to even the harshest and most forbidding climates of tropical

America—Cartagena, Panama, Guayaquil, and the like—was a Spanish feat achieved with the few technical aids available in the sixteenth and seventeenth centuries. A visitor to the Venezuelan plains—a rugged region of abrupt temperature changes, sharply contrasting with the benign climate of the Andean zone and of the hills and valleys along the coast—cannot fail to admire the evidence of Spain's city-building enterprise in the now decaying settlements at Barinas, San Carlos, Ospino, and Guanare. The strong stamp of Hispanic tradition is visible in the churches built in an excellent baroque or neoclassic eighteenth-century style and in the picturesque Andalusian character of the private dwellings of those localities whose inhabitants later preferred more congenial climates. By the end of the colonial period this cultural impulse had penetrated into such remote and inaccessible parts of South America as the upper Orinoco and the forests of northern Paraguay. This fact needs to be explained, not just for the sake of the academic Hispanism so dear to the conservative classes of Spanish America, or for the sake of any spirit of colonialism, but rather because we came into Western civilization through Spanish forms. Even the rightful demands of the mixed masses of Spanish America for social reform and a better standard of living must be stated in Spanish to be truly valid and effective. Through the dissolution of the native empires and the acquisition of a new, common language, Spanish America exists as a historical unit that did not break into mutually suspicious and fiercely antagonistic fragments. Spanish is an admirable symbol of political independence in our historical evolution, because—owing to the work of Bolívar and San Martín and to a background of shared history in the wars against Ferdinand VII—it was this language medium that prevented our becoming another Africa for nineteenth-century imperial powers to carve. In world geography today no group of peoples enjoys within itself this powerful bond of family relationship—not even the Balkans or the British Commonwealth, scattered as it is over several continents. Although they wave different flags, a Chilean is much closer in an emotional sense to a Mexican than an Australian is to a Canadian. This deep relationship accounts for a common historical culture even though the former political cohesion has been broken since the nineteenth century.

PSYCHOLOGY OF THE SPANISH UNDERTAKING

This is not the occasion to bring up again the stale legal and moral question of the validity or nonvalidity of the Spanish Conquest. A demon of destruction did not always possess the conquistadors, as the Black Legend would have it, nor were they saints or knights on a spiritual crusade, as the no less ingenuous White Legend would have it. The cruelty of such psychotic personalities as Lope de Aguirre and Carvajal—"Demons of the Andes" as they were called—on whom the harsh nature of tropical America and the terrible solitude of their wanderings had wreaked havoc, even robbing them of all scruples, is assuredly not comparable to the calculated fear that the great soldier and statesman Hernán Cortés now and then had to impose on his foes contrary to his conciliatory and diplomatic temperament.

A splendid Spanish virtue is frankness. The conquistadors themselves recorded, with a certain soldierly bluntness, the "all too human" character of the Conquest. In one of his long dispatches Cortés wrote: "We Spaniards are overbearing and insistent." Elsewhere he commented on his difficult role of a statesman who must appease the greed and impatience of his followers while avoiding any sign of weakness in maintaining authority in the face of the Indians. Again Cortés expressed himself admirably in an apt estimate of the social nature of the Conquest: "Now, if every Spaniard in these parts and those who come hither were clergymen, or if their main purpose were to convert the natives, I am quite certain that their association with the Indians would be very beneficial; but, since the reverse is true, the effect of their actions is the reverse, for it is a well-known fact that most of the Spaniards who come here are low, hardened types much given to every kind of vice and sin. If they were allowed to move about freely among the Indian villages, they would—God save the mark!—convert the natives to their vices rather than to virtue." But there is a favorable side to the violence of the Conquest: the stout, heroic courage with which many of these men from the very dregs of society performed their difficult task has a positive significance in history. López de Gómara's chronicle possesses the beauty of the finest epic when he describes how the conquistadors at Trujillo, Peru, greeted Viceroy Blasco Núñez Vela, who had come to enforce the New Laws designed to limit their power to restrict the authority that they had won by adventurous swords. Confronted by the cold impersonality of the law that failed to distinguish between a hero and a loafer and that would reduce everyone to the same level, members of that group of weather-beaten veterans of heroic campaigns, according to López de Gómara, "displayed their toothless gums from living on toasted corn throughout the conquest of Peru, others uncovered their many wounds and stone bruises, and still others showed large bites of alligators."

It has been said *ad nauseam* that the chief concern of the Spanish Conquest was the quest of gold, in which respect it was after all no different than any other conquest made by Europeans. Long centuries before it ever occurred to Karl Marx, the archpriest of Hita had declared in his jocular, sometimes vulgar, and very Spanish way that the primary drive of every person "is to get a good living." If even velvet-clad gentlemen of Queen Elizabeth's court struggled for gold in exotic adventures of conquest—as, for example, Sir Walter Raleigh, who tried to create for himself a kind of personal Peru in Guiana—why should we be astonished that a gang of commoners, members of an impoverished lower nobility, and disinherited bastards who formed a tidal wave of conquerors should have their dreams of treasure islands? Sancho Panza's dream that Cervantes incorporated into Spain's most representative book—the dream of a hearty meal, of a continuous wedding feast with a roast ceaselessly turning on the spit and wine flowing freely—was the eternal theme and constant illusion of the Spanish people. From the time of Charles V the great estates of the *mesta* (union of cattle raisers) prevailed over the former economy of small farms in Castile, and the nation embarked on foreign adventures to the detriment of its internal economic order.

One kind of "rascality" on the part of the needy masses was emigration to Spanish America. Even Cervantes, the great interpreter of Spain's inner being, would seek to end his days at Soconusco, at La Paz in Bolivia, or at Cartagena in Colombia, as a magistrate among the Indians or as a clerk of the royal treasury. In spite of the perils of an unknown and untamed land, stout-hearted individuals among the humble masses expected, somewhat paradoxically, to find a security in the New World that evaded them in the Old World. It was even a way to acquire aristocratic status, as Francisco Pizarro said on one occasion according to López de Gómara, adding that for their efforts those who went to the Indies deserved "as many exemptions and distinctions as the heroes who helped the king, Don Pelayo, to regain Spain from the Moors."

Even accepting the pursuit of gold as the ideal, the Spaniard loved the adventure of the quest almost more than its monetary value. Distasteful to him were purely commercial enterprises like the Portuguese colonies in Asia or later those of the English that were primarily coastal trading posts where the natives brought their wares from the interior to be weighed, measured, and haggled over. To achieve eminence, to become a nobleman in the *ricohombre* class, and to wield influence in affairs of state—these were the real reasons why he craved gold. "Money makes quality," the Spanish satirist Francisco Quevedo would declare. A series of medieval qualms inhibited the Spanish soul from acquiring the capitalistic consciousness that was beginning to take hold of northern Europe. These scruples stemmed from age-old preachments of scholastic theology against money and against lending at interest and also from a disdain for commercial transactions and money-making, which in Spain had been regarded as an occupation suitable only for humble Jews. Indeed, the whole literature of the classic period exudes the haughtiest kind of contempt for capitalistic activities. Moral discourses of the time are filled with vituperation flung at the Genoese, the Ligurians, Lombards, Flemings, and all the Europeans who had made progress in developing financial operations. In the seventeenth century the *pícaro* [rogue] became a popular figure largely because of his defiant attitude toward what we today call the bourgeois order or the capitalistic organization. The economic outlook of the *pícaro* was essentially one of adventure or chance, and hence it scarcely differed from that of the conquistador. In no page of literature is this antimodern attitude of the Spanish spirit so plainly stated—its opposition to evil and corrupting wealth and its hostility to a love of comfort that robs men of their manhood—as in Francisco de Quevedo's celebrated *Satirical and Censorious Epistle*, a veritable model of the Spanish ethos.

As a consequence, there was in our beginnings a kind of undeveloped economic sense and a disdain for the pragmatic and utilitarian currents rising in northern Europe and destined to reach a high point in nineteenth-century industrialization and its machine culture, which would leave us far behind in the great technological adventure of modern times. Possibly it was the Spaniard's proud and at times haughty consciousness of his virile nature that made him rebel against the machine. His medieval spirit moved him to prefer the fighter to the merchant and his soul to his body. Hispanic peoples are still unacquainted with capitalism in its fullest development.

If the incentive of gold in the conquering expeditions has been stressed at some length, it would be well to consider other drives—such as the pursuit of glory, for example—which, according to the classical definition of Jacob Burckhardt, was one of the deepest longings of Renaissance man. In yearning for fame the Spanish conquistador clearly embodied the Renaissance spirit of individualism. This is especially true because the Hispanic mind, still steeped in the moral and religious principles of the Middle Ages, believed that earthly fame could sometimes be harmonized with glory in heaven. Hernán Cortés illustrates this dualism in one of his letters: "Once standing where they could not see me, I overheard some of my men in a shack discussing whether I was insane and had put myself into a position from which I could not escape. This idea was conveyed to me a good many times, and I always cheered them by saying that the largest realms and dominions in the world were tributary to Your Majesty. For this reason we were gaining glory in the next world while in this one we were winning the highest honor and reward received by any generation down to our time." Today, after several centuries of encyclopedic learning and higher criticism, this may cause us to smile, or perhaps we may consider it mere rhetoric for a man of such worldly power as Cortés to talk about glory in heaven. But it must be remembered that the Spanish Conquest sought its legal and religious justification in spreading the Gospel, and to Spanish sensibility there was nothing incongruous in the idea of a fighting saint—a "saint in armor"—and a good cavalryman. Had not the religious imagination of the Spaniard converted the worship of the Apostle Saint James into a martial myth? Was not Spain the home of the great fighting preacher Domingo de Guzmán? And was not Ignacio de Loyola's militant Jesuit order to rise in that same sixteenth century? If a Saint Hernán Cortés seems an absurdity to us today, it was far less so in his own time.

If in one respect the sixteenth-century Spaniard was very close to Italy, and, indeed, had penetrated too deeply for the strong, worldly perfume of the Italian Renaissance to cling to him, nevertheless its ideas found a soil in Spain rich in the equally strong ethical, chivalric, and religious principles of the Middle Ages. Therefore sixteenth-century Spain did not bring forth such amoral personalities and pagans as abounded in Italy or such a free and easy individualism; rather, it produced beings who reconciled the so-called Faustian longing of the Renaissance with a moral and religious system deriving from scholasticism and the popular ethics still so vigorous in Spain. The conquistadors were not men of the Middle Ages as so frequently asserted, nor were they entirely of the Renaissance. They were borderline men who exemplified Spain's transition from one age to the other. Medieval was their scorn for the techniques of trade, as we have seen, and for organized commercial enterprise. Renaissance were the emblem *Plus ultra* surmounting their ships and also the restlessness and hunger for more knowledge and broader horizons which impelled Cortés to forsake the comfortable enjoyment of his gains and to push on into the wild Hibueras country. These things also drove the septuagenarian Gonzalo Jiménez de Quesada to turn his back on the settlement he had founded at Santa Fe de Bogotá, on his marshalship, and on his respected civilian rank to make a grueling march through tropical lowlands. When he had apparently freed himself forever from Indian arrows, from the wild tangle of jungle vegetation, from snakes and dismal swamps, he plunged into them again as if lured to their perils by nostalgia. Inseparable from a Sancho Panza enjoyment of winnings was the eternal quixotic passion for adventure. Hardly any conquistador managed to enjoy the full extent of his success; the spoils fell to the Spanish American oligarchies of government officials or merchants coming late in the colonial period, notably the Basques, rather than to these first arrivals—the soldiers who had won the land by their swords. Incidentally, these were the same oligarchies that the nineteenth-century revolution for independence would confront.

Then again, the fighter was conquered by his conquest. He succumbed to the charm and beauty of the land, as Cortés did, and his acquisitive drive yielded to the more sedentary one to settle down and take root. The social impulse to found a family, to become respectable, and to rise to the aristocratic rank of a *ricohombre* triumphed over the previous urge for adventure. It is well, perhaps, in the story of the conquest of Venezuela, to compare the contrasting behavior of Spaniards like Losada, Díaz Moreno, and Villegas with that of the German representatives of the business house of the Welsers, whose presence in the western part of the country left such a frightful memory of plunder and massacre. From the outset the Spaniards were bent on founding cities, but the Germans destroyed the few existing hamlets; in seeking the El Dorado from these primitive centers of settlement, the Germans plunged into the interior and waged ruthless war on the natives. A German promoter like Alfinger seemed the archtype of cruelty to even the hardened sixteenth-century Spanish soldiers engaged in such an extremely difficult conquest as the one in Venezuela. The tropics and the fierce attacks of the Indians exerted on these German bookkeepers and accountants a more brutalizing and regressive effect—indeed one that was more destructive of a moral sense—than it did upon the whole mass of the Spanish soldiers, most of whom were of course illiterate.

THE SOCIAL COMPLEX AND
SPANISH AND EUROPEAN VALUES

The conquistador's instinct was not always merely a drive or a force in a vacuum, but it also acted in conjunction with what may be called the social complex of his time—that is, the sum total of ideas, collective sentiments, and ethical standards. If a history compiled from purely public documentation were inadequate, even less satisfactory would be one with biographical data added which failed to include such abstract or intangible material. When an analysis of the Conquest is attempted, the prevailing notions of the time concerning the nature of the world and man and his destiny are as important a part of the problem as the adventures of Cortés and Pizarro. We cannot cut the umbilical cord linking our history to the sixteenth-century Hispanic world. It is a paradox of some of the personalities of the Conquest that at the same time they expend tremendous energy on it they try to justify or explain themselves within the accepted framework of ideas. Even such a thoroughgoing bandit as Lope de Aguirre—certainly one of the most satanic figures of the Conquest—in a letter to Philip II, censured the friars who were taking their ease instead of proselyting and the magistrates who were not administering justice. It was not merely a matter of dissimulation, or of hypocrisy, or a kind self-assured duplicity, as rationalistic critics would later assert, but, rather, an echo of the social complex—the accepted canons of the time.

Rufino Blanco Fombona has brilliantly described the conquistadors as extremely liberated personalities, lusty specimens of humanity who reveled in their strength and seemed to break all norms of conduct, like the heroes starving for action and excitement in a *fin de siècle* decadence made fashionable at the close of the nineteenth century. On the other hand, the North American writer Charles Lumnis, with a certain sanctimonious piety, depicts them in quite opposite terms in his arraignment of the Black Legend of Spanish cruelty and obscurantism. The "all too human" traits of the conquerors never broke entirely with the whole set of moral traditions and religious values brought over from the old country. The real historical problem is in the individual's conflict with, or respect for, the exisiting patterns of his time. Still another paradox of Spanish culture must be noted. Whole new systems of criticism and values in politics, economics, religion, war, and science were beginning to penetrate Europe when Spain was engaged in its great overseas adventure. Machiavelli and other Italian thinkers were breaking down the medieval relationship between two worlds—the temporal and the divine—and between religion and politics which seemed to persist in the close association of Church and state in Spain during the sixteenth and seventeenth centuries. The concept of the state as a secular arm of the Church and the sovereign as the sword of the Faith dominated Spanish policies at the moment when a flexible and secularized diplomacy of the French king, Francis I, was flirting with the Moslems and hoping to win the support of the sultan. In the Spanish pattern of Church and state—which President García Moreno of Ecuador would revive in a strange manner in the nineteenth century—the sovereign was aiding the divine plan because, according to the theory, in the temporal sphere a person's salvation depended upon the way he prepared himself on earth to win a place in heaven. Free inquiry in religious matters broke upon the rock of authority that safeguarded order. In the struggle with Luther, the moral principles of Protestantism did not trouble Catholic theologians so much as did its excessive religious particularism. In contrast to Roman Catholic discipline, the Nordic world claimed the right to an inner experience, to interpret sacred literature and to simplify liturgy and the ecclesiastical hierarchy. Like the Hussites of Bohemia, it wished to drink from the chalice reserved to the priest. To all this the Catholic Church and Philip II reacted as a modern conservative government might react to workers' demands regarded as outrageous or to the slogans of a party on the extreme left: "It is the end of law and order! It is revolution!" The Spanish state, as the secular arm of the last and impossible religious crusade, stood against a revolution erupting from the very core of the modern world, and it bled itself white in the strife of the Counter Reformation. With fierce and obstinate pride, it turned its back on the new developments in science, economics, and technology which were beginning to alter European culture. Like a misanthropic emperor whose vast power was ebbing away in disillusionment and want of esteem, the Spanish state was presiding over its own dissolution.

That was the negative—the dark and ineffective—side of our Hispanic heritage. It was Spain's misfortune to be judged by the later criteria of values that produced capitalism, the lay state, and the rejection of policies stemming from the "universal principles" of the Middle Ages in favor of those based on naked acts and brute force. Its spiritual world stood aloof from the dynamics of modern history: the Protestant freedom of inquiry, experimentalism, the ideas of the Encyclopedia, and the positivism and materialism of the nineteenth century. I think, however, that we can comprehend and evaluate our Spanish heritage outside both the conservative thesis of Church and state and that of nineteenth-century liberalism, which scorned or denied whatever disagreed with the cult of industrialization, as is so clearly evident in the sociology of Herbert Spencer. The spiritual crisis itself of that period moves us to view with calmer eyes some of the older values of Hispanic culture. On the border land where the violence of the conquistador and the ethical humanism of the Laws of the Indies meet and where Las Casas battled the Spanish overlords, we come nearer—above and beyond all propaganda—the reality of our beginnings.

If the new political science starting with Machiavelli was to lead, as in the Pan-Germanic type of historiography, to the glorification of the accomplished fact, to the success theory, and to a monstrous racism whose foulest manifestation appeared in Nazi Germany, Spanish culture can surely claim a moral idealism drawn from early theological and traditional sources (Saint Augustine, Saint Thomas Aquinas, the legal ideas of the *fueros* [local charters], and the *Siete Partidas* [Seven Parts] of Alphonso the Wise), which is visible in the legislation for the Indies. Spanish culture has a further claim to moral idealism when it is recalled that great thinkers such as Suárez and Vitoria, pursuing other paths than those of Protestant thought, laid the foundations of a modern theory of the Christian state. In contrast to the separation of morality and politics urged by advocates of the powerful state, the ideal of Spain was the effort to integrate the ethical and the social. It demanded that facts should show their credentials of logic, soundness, and relation to abstract justice. Owing to this kind of thought, a debate of such resounding importance as the one between Las Casas and Sepúlveda about the Conquest of America could take place, even against Spain's own immediate interests; and owing to this philosophy, Father Vitoria could advocate a system of international law above nation or state in his famous treatise *De Potestate Ecclesiae* and in his commentaries on Saint Thomas Aquinas. Would such a polemic be possible in a modern totalitarian state to which, with incredible historical nearsightedness, the Spain of Charles V and Philip II has occasionally been compared?

If, from the point of view of positivistic science, scholasticism shackled Spanish thought until well into the eighteenth century and removed it from the most dynamic influences of modern history, from another—possibly higher and less utilitarian—standpoint it helped to give Spanish life its firm moral pattern, its philosophy of behavior, by which the genius of the race managed to reconcile chivalry with Christianity, as is so brilliantly symbolized in the figure of Don Quixote. Almost as if he were a contemporary of the great theologians at the University of Salamanca, Don Miguel Antonio Caro, a remarkable humanist of Spanish America, similarly rationalized that timeless concept of justice in the nineteenth century by declaring:

> When a fact neither possesses, admits, nor accepts any basis and is alleged as a sole reason, it is an insult to true reason. It would be arrogance and madness to demand the ultimate explanation of things, but it is the inherent right of rational creatures to require facts to present their credentials as manifestations or agents of higher forces. For a fact to claim my rational respect I demand that it rest substantially, though not in every detail, upon a preëxistent law or that it be linked with that law in some way even when I do not fathom its ultimate causes. When we pass from the causal to the providential, when from

what *is* we rise to what *ought to be*—when, in short, we leave chaos and enter into order which is all light and warmth—the heart naturally rejoices and the mind is calm and quiet.

That *ought to be*, in the ethical tradition of Spain doubtlessly tempered the fury of the Conquest and likewise promoted the work of spreading the Gospel.

Along with the military effort there was a practical humanism unhampered by dreams of beauty as it was in the Italian Renaissance and one that was animated by a yearning for social betterment; there was a desire to make amends for the conquistador's crimes, to teach and to protect the helpless masses as was so well exemplified in the work of Vasco de Quiroga, Motolinía, and Luis de Valdivia. All this constitutes a still vital legacy—and one of the highest solvency—in the cultural and moral life of Hispanic America.

From European to a Mixed Culture

IV

European culture first permeated Spanish American in the urban centers established in the sixteenth century, although the peculiarities of the surroundings, as will presently be noted, quickly imposed modifications. In Santo Domingo, the first Spanish settlement in the New World, where the conqueror found no native tradition worth preserving and where the Indian element was absorbed almost imperceptibly into the alien, the problems of acculturation differed markedly from those in a region such as Mexico where the indigenous components would successfully struggle for incorporation or transformation in the over-all Spanish pattern.

Founded in 1494, Santo Domingo—the first seaport, stronghold, capital, and center of gravity of the Conquest overseas—was the last and most remote outpost of fifteenth-century Spanish culture, with its waning Gothic and incipient Renaissance influences. There Don Diego Columbus, eldest son of the discoverer and the second Admiral of the Ocean Sea, tried to set up a miniature court in the manner of a Renaissance prince. "From the outset," wrote Pedro Henríquez de Ureña, "the Spaniard aspired to live like a lord on the toil of the Indians and Negroes." Don Diego's recent elevation into the aristocracy, thanks to the courage, genius, and luck of the discoverer, had linked him to the bluest blood of Castile through his marriage to a niece of the Duke of Alba, María de Toledo, who accompanied him to the Indies together with a magnificent retinue of officials and lackeys. From the lofty height of a tower built by the military architect Cristóbal de Tapia in imitation of similar structures in Spain in which a castellan took an oath to defend the castle with his life, and later from a fortified castle—the accepted form of palace-residence in the fifteenth century—Don Diego endeavored to give his New World capital an air of lordly pomp and circumstance. He was fond of books and art objects, and in his social circle he included the future historian of the Indies, Gonzalo Fernández de Oviedo. Indeed, it was remarkable that this spendthrift, uneconomical, and effete mode of life found a foothold there. Considering the difficulties of the days following the discovery and the relative unimportance of the island, the city of Santo Domingo began to flourish with certain splendor.

The ancient Latin tradition of cities laid out in a rectangular pattern, which the Renaissance preference for simple, straight lines had revived, was renewed in the early New World communities. The layout of a town, the ceremonies preceding its foundation, its basic architectural features (a central square, arcades, a church, and a jail)—a scheme, indeed, that resembled a checkerboard—were all set forth precisely in Book IV, paragraphs 7 and 8 of the Laws of the Indies. Carefully studied was every detail, such as the public square or polygonal area "adequate for parades on horseback or other general spectacles" and of a "size commensurate with the population," main streets with "arcades for the convenience of tradesmen," and the location of the principal buildings with relation to prevailing winds, whether warm or cold from off the coast or the mountains. Local pride, the desire for distinction, and a separate identity were satisfied by granting coats of arms, emblems, banners, pennants, flags, and special seals. In the cultural mores of our colonial ancestors, historical events—such as the date of the founding of the town, or when the Spaniards settled in the locality after defeating the Indians—became almost sacred occasions for observance with symbolic ceremonies as, for example, the "parade of the banner." Even with the advent of the republic in 1821 the City of Mexico continued to celebrate Saint Hypolite's day—August 13—as the anniversary of the final battle between the Spaniards and the Aztec, the defeat of Cuauhtémoc, and the definite occupation of Tenochtitlán by Hernán Cortés. In Lima a similar commemoration coincided with the Day of the Magi Kings—January 6. On such festive occasions "rich and majestic hangings draped the balconies," "the cream of society came forth in bright uniforms mounted on handsome, gaily caparisoned steeds," while others displayed arms and weapons "that were more revered for being dented and old than brand new ones," and through the city streets a marshal, "in full, resplendent regalia and astride an armored horse," bore the standard "on red velvet cushions with golden tassles and lace trimmings." From the very beginning of our history the ruling class imposed an ornate style of urban existence despite the poverty and backwardness of the locality. It offered a curious combination of allegory, medieval formalism, and Renaissance luxury with an admixture of Indian and *mestizo* elements, especially in Mexico, Peru, and Guatemala.

Fourteen years after its founding, Santo Domingo had already become a thoroughly Spanish city with convents, schools, and a bishopric. The Laws of the Indies stipulated as an indispensable requirement "that every city in Spanish America should evoke wonder in the Indians when they saw it so that they would thereby understand that the Spaniards were permanently settled there and, accordingly, should be feared and respected, their friendship sought, and no offense to be given." Alonso Rodríguez, the chief architect of the cathedral in the Andalusian city of Seville, had signed a contract to direct from that distance the buildings to be constructed in the new city by the artisans and quarrymen whose presence in the Indies is noted as early as 1510. The *encomenderos* [feudal overlords] liberally supplied tribute in the sixteenth century to pay for erecting the churches and convents of San Nicolás, Santo Domingo, Santa Clara, and San Francisco, all structures of solid masonry in styles varying from Isabellan Gothic to the Renaissance regularity of square compartments. As if to accentuate the close connection between the recently discovered lands and Renaissance Europe, it fell to the Italian humanist Alexander Geraldini, who was appointed the second bishop of Santo Domingo, to lay the cornerstone of the cathedral in Santo Domingo in 1523 and to celebrate the event in a pompous Latin poem. Bishop Geraldini, a protégé of Pope Leo X and an epicurean spirit somewhat out of his element in that Caribbean world, ordered the coat of arms of the Medici engraved on the cathedral. He also asked the architect Rodrigo Gil de Liendo to carve a frieze in the most classic Italian style on the wide cornice, and to decorate the choir loft in a graceful Florentine pattern in which seven cherubs lifting their voices heavenward symbolized the notes of the old musical scale.

Aristocrats and clergymen capable of enjoying such refinements were dwelling by that time in Santo Domingo. Gonzalo Fernández de Oviedo was using his leisure as a castellan of the fort to gather material for his voluminous *History of the Indies,* which describes the fauna and flora of this new area, and he was also jotting down the eight-syllable learned verses of his *Quincuagenarias.* Life at this seaport was enlivened by the adventures of men who had been on the Isle of Pearls or on the mainland to the west. The mystery of the still-undiscovered lands lured venturesome spirits who regarded Santo Domingo as merely the gateway to the wonders of the New World.

The great expectations of wealth and heroic deeds entertained by the first settlers seemed to justify the relative luxury and the elaborate ornamentation of the churches and monasteries of the primate city. "The grain for the harvest is great," declared soldiers and friars alike. But this first European community in the New World was to be troubled also by some of the great problems that the Renaissance stirred in the Western conscience. The great debates over the justice of colonial expansion and of Indian slavery, which became serious concerns of Spanish ethics in the sixteenth century, began in Santo Domingo earlier than they did anywhere else. From 1510 Friar Antonio de Montesinos preached there against the Spanish overlords, and thus started a great moral campaign that found its most eminent leader in Bartolomé de las Casas. In convents elsewhere, other clergymen were similarly at work—such as Friar Tomás de San Martín, later famous for his evangelistic work in Peru, who wrote a long *Opinion on Whether the Property of Conquerors, Settlers, and*

Overlords was Properly Acquired, and Friar Tomás de Ortiz, whose *Curious Account of the Life, Laws, Customs, and Rites of the Indians* began the splendid task of ethnological description destined to be one of the greatest achievements of missionary literature. An echo of the fierce religious and theological disputes that brought on the violent schism of the Reformation also reached these distant shores. Around 1513 the stormy figure of Father Carlos de Aragón, later a victim of the Inquisition, whose antischolastic preachings assailed the Thomistic system and the medieval concept of authority, passed through Santo Domingo. A few years later the literary circle of the Andalusian poet Lázaro Bejarano would harbor the subversive humanism of Erasmus, with its ideas of free inquiry, tolerance, and the condemnation of war. In mid-sixteenth-century Santo Domingo this same poet, with a satirical flair reminiscent of Erasmus, would write against the concept of authority and its perfectionism in his *Purgatory of Love,* a kind of "madman's ship" account of early colonial life. And when Bejarano was summoned before the Inquisition, he would endeavor to establish the principle of "divine illumination" by which pre-Protestant criticism opposed the concept of Catholic authority. The early and surreptitious current of Erasmian thought, which was so fruitful in sixteenth-century Spanish life, was reflected in the colonies. Tracing its movement through Inquisitional records and the devotional literature of the time is still an unexplored field of investigation in the history of our culture. As Marcel Bataillon's exhaustive study of Erasmian thought in Spain has shown, the *Inquiridion* was one of the most influential models of the Spanish Renaissance. Even when the rapid importance of Santo Domingo in the colonial world began to decline as a result of the explorations on the mainland and the extraordinary lure offered by Mexico's wider and richer fields of adventure, a curious residue of culture lingered on in that city. As late as the middle of the eighteenth century, students from Cuba, Venezuela, and the Atlantic coast of Colombia attended the University of Santo Tomás, which had been founded in 1538 and was controlled by the Dominican order. In the eighteenth century, Santo Domingo would supply teachers for the universities of Havana and Caracas, just as its early Franciscan and Dominican convents had extended the work of conversion into Mexico, northern South America, and even into distant Peru.

THE CULTURAL PROBLEM OF THE
MEXICAN CONQUEST

Still more complex is the problem of European "transculturation"— to employ a useful neologism of the Cuban sociologist Fernando Ortiz—in the wealthy and legendary lands of Mexico and Peru. *The Biography of Don Juan de Zumárraga, First Bishop and Archbishop of Mexico*, by the eminent Mexican scholar García Icazbalceta, and his equally useful study of public instruction in sixteenth-century Mexico City give us a picture of the problems confronting the Spaniard when military conquest began to yield to political and ecclesiastical organization and it was necessary to bring the exotic world of the Aztec into Spain's imperial system. Dating from early times is the still-unresolved conflict of Spanish American culture. On the one hand, the cultivated classes, always a little out of touch with reality about them, tried diligently to transplant and imitate the most elaborate ways of European living. On the other hand, a few exceptional friars and missionaries—such as Vasco de Quiroga, Pedro de Gante, and Sahagún—intuitively realized that ideas other than the purely European were necessary to reach the soul of the aboriginal elements. More suitable methods, for example, were needed for teaching the natives to improve their own trades and crafts, for studying their languages, and for helping them to express their own unique personalities. Still valid today is the academic thinking of these early missionaries—especially of Sahagún and Motolinía, who identified themselves completely with the Indians and who reëducated themselves to a certain extent by this association. The valuable experience of sixteenth-century Mexico should not be forgotten in the policies of present-day Peru, Guatemala, Ecuador, Bolivia, and Mexico itself, which are attempting to assimilate their Indian population.

In Icazbalceta's biography of Zumárraga we can glimpse the cultural problems agitating Mexico City soon after the military phase of the Conquest. The ecclesiastical authorities, seeking the peaceful subjugation of the natives, struggled against the greed and cupidity of the royal judges, who—like the infamous Nuño de Guzmán—preferred ruthless exploitation. The men of God clashed with haughty, feudal-minded overlords, and the presence of the indefatigable Bartolomé de las Casas is noted in the first assembly of the Mexican bishops in 1546 after his valiant battle in Spain in behalf of the Indians. There he won that stout "Declaration of the Rights of the Indians" with which the episcopal synod confronted the secular masters. This document read in part:

> All unbelievers, whatever their sect or religion and whatever their state of sin, by Natural and Divine Law and by the birthright of all peoples, properly possess and hold domain over the things they have acquired without detriment to others, and with equal right they are entitled to their principalities, realms, states, honors, jurisdictions, and dominions. War against unbelievers for the purpose of subjecting them to Christian control, and to compell them by this means to accept the Christian faith and religion, or to remove obstacles to this end that may exist, is reckless, unjust, perverse, and tyrannical. The sole and definitive reason of the Papacy for granting the supreme rule and imperial sovereignty of the Indies to the monarchs of Castile and Leon was to preach the Gospel, spread the Faith, and convert the inhabitants; it was not to make these monarchs richer princes or greater lords than they already were.

Along with the clash of spiritual and political authority in the realm of ideas went the practical problems of Indian conversion. These included baptism, community organization according to the Christian family pattern, providing parishes, missions, and missionary schools, and eliminating the natural fear that close association with the Spaniards inevitably aroused in the natives. To harmonize contrasting societies and worlds of the haughty conqueror and the timorous Indian was, in the mind of Zumárraga, a difficult task of balance and justice which properly devolved upon the Church. If the spiritual power for making peace was not strengthened along with the war-making power—Hernán Cortés, with the intuition of a great statesman, had fully appreciated this—the true subjugation of the Indian masses was unattainable. When the first Franciscans reached

Mexico City in 1524 Cortés met them on his knees at the city gates, kissed the mantles of the barefoot friars, and begged their blessings, as if to bestow all the respect of his authority and the obeisance of his sword upon the new moral force that had come to assert itself. It was then the intention of Cortés—oddly coinciding with that of an ecclesiastical organizer such as Zumárraga—that the Spaniard should not regard the Mexican land as merely the scene of a passing military adventure but rather as a place in which to settle and take root, and for the Indians to coöperate in the formation of a new society. Zumárraga had to concern himself with both his episcopal duties and such elementary matters of domestic economy as having a boatload of seeds and fruit trees brought from Spain which, when planted in Mexico—as he wrote in a delightful letter to the emperor —"would make the settlers stop whining about their homesickness for Castile, whose fruits they miss more than anything else." In another letter he submitted to the king a complete proposal for the economic development of his vast bishopric designed to discourage the Spaniards from "stuffing themselves here and going home to Spain to empty themselves." He requested that large quantities of flax-seed and hemp be sent along with competent persons to cultivate and process them, because cordage manufactured in Mexico would be needed for ships sailing the Pacific. In spite of the religious prejudices of the time, he urged that Moorish families be sent from Granada to make the first plantings and set up the first looms, thus facilitating the cultivation of the mulberry tree and the silk industry in Mexico. He also ordered the naturalist Alonso de Figuerola, Precentor of Oaxaca, to write a book of instruction for the Indians on the cultivation, weaving, and dyeing of silk. Zumárraga dreamed also of abolishing the drudgery of the *tamemes*, the proletarian Indians, whom the Aztec used as beasts of burden, by distributing mules and donkeys among them. The Spaniards took good care of the horses used in warfare and for personal display. Therefore the Indians, the bishop reflected, ought to be obliged to own donkeys and sheep.

The earliest adaptations to the demands of the new environment upon the regime of the conqueror; came out of this direct and active contact of the friars and missionaries with the real nature of the country. In that early stage of Spanish American communities two cultures were to exist side by side, especially in Mexico and Peru. One was aristocratic in character, and its enjoyment was the lot claimed by descendants of the first founders and wealthiest families, the upper secular clergy, and—toward the end of the sixteenth century—by the Jesuits. The other was a humbler and more utilitarian culture developed by the Franciscans and later by the Dominicans and Augustinians through their first-hand association with the aboriginal world. This latter culture left an indelible mark on the architecture, cathechistic literature, and pictographic and decorative arts. It also left a precious heritage in the wonderful exploration of the Indian soul through the genius of such men as Sahagún and, in an exceedingly interesting social and economic utopia, the handiwork of Vasco de Quiroga.

RENAISSANCE PATTERNS IN SIXTEENTH-CENTURY MEXICO

The purely European character of the culture in the first century of colonial life is evident in the artistic and literary creations, which could interest only the small ruling class; to the common people the nature of these writings was entirely remote and incomprehensible, and they were useless for missionary endeavors. The University of Mexico, founded in 1553, attracted what might be called a lettered elite: such famous theologians and canonists as Friar Alonso de la Veracruz, such Latinists and Hellenists as Doctor Frías, and rhetoricians and logicians trained at famous institutions of Spain such as the universities of Salamanca and Alcalá. The personalities of these individuals may be partly glimpsed in the interesting dialogues in Latin by Francisco Cervantes de Salazar which offer a testimonial of great importance to Mexican intellectual life about 1554.

A friend and possibly a pupil of Juan Luis Vives in Spain, Cervantes de Salazar composed these dialogues to familiarize his students with a graceful style of Latin conversation on topics and events of the day, following the unexcelled model provided by Erasmus. Departing from the cloistered halls of the university, the author describes the main thoroughfares and buildings of Mexico City and, at eventide, brings his stroll to an end in the quiet groves of Chapultepec, which Viceroy Luis de Velasco had converted into a public park. Enthusiastic about architectural styles, an avid reader of Vitruvius, and trained in the purest Renaissance esthetics, Cervantes de Salazar sings the praises not only of the literature flourishing in Mexico City but also of its public edifices built in accordance with the tenets of an older architecture. He notes, for example, that the columns of the viceroy's palace are rounded, as Vitrubius recommends, that the "right proportion is maintained between their height and girth," and that the architraves are neatly carved. The spacious halls of the viceregal palace remind him of the Roman *procestria*. It pleases him that the great lords of the city have built houses of cut stone which are carefully plumbed, thus conveying a feeling of harmony and beauty. All his poetic instinct is revealed in the final, graceful pages devoted to the woods around Chapultepec "with their leafy beauty," where lovely springs gush forth in such limpid clarity "that in spite of their depth the tiny pebbles on the bottom are visible." One of the most moving passages in the entire dialogue is his eulogy of clear, pure water. Agreeing with the judgment of Hippocrates and Avicena, he regards it as "the most like air, which warms and chills most rapidly, is lightest and most health-giving, because it sparkles in unsullied pools." From the height of Chapultepec he is enchanted by the cool freshness of the landscape of the lofty valley of Mexico, which the Spaniards have already begun to dot with spires and towers. All that is needed to endow this scene with the classic beauty of southern Europe is the olive trees and the grapevines that yielded those delightful complements of Old World living: olive oil and wine. Well beyond the towers and palaces of red porous stone, built by the conquistadors now turned nobles, the strange, mysterious native elements live in the tortuous suburbs, which contrast with the symmetry of the newer streets of the city, or much farther away over the hills. And the humanist author who, a few pages back, has praised the Spanish schools and colleges that are beginning to accept Indian and half-caste pupils, cherishes the belief that Mexico may fulfill the Greek dream of a "microcosm," a synthesis, or a harmonious fusion of two opposite worlds. At the end of the book, and in the true Renaissance manner, the publisher and printer Juan Pablos de Brescia apologizes for the fact that it was not "printed in more graceful type, with better spelling, and in larger format." The printing press had functioned in Mexico City since 1539, and designs and allegorical figures characteristic of the period already adorned the title pages of Mexican books.

Lyric poetry and the epic, along with the Latin dialogues used in the university, were to be the favorite literary genres of the Europeanizing minority in the sixteenth century. Thanks to the influence of Ariosto—whose *Orlando Furioso* provided a synthesis of the formal refinements of Renaissance literature, the mixing of the mythological and the contemporary, the psychological and the merely narrative—it becomes difficult to discern any clear boundaries between the epic and the lyric in sixteenth-century poetry. The martial and the idyllic spirits tend to alternate in the epic poems of the time.

At the same time that the University of Mexico was opening its doors a gentleman- and soldier-poet at the extreme southern end of the hemisphere was creating the first modern epic on an American theme. In royal octaves, after the manner of Ariosto and with the mingling of reality and mythology, he etched the figures of the wild Araucanian Indians with the foreshortened precision of a classic relief. Because his theme was new and—like the *Lusiads* of Camoëns —his poem was one of the first epics inspired by the modern adventures of Western man and thus broke through the space limits of ancient classical culture, Ercilla apologizes for the elements of extreme novelty and crudity in his work:

> Not of ladies, love, or graces
> do I sing, nor knights enamored,
> nor of gifts and shows of feeling,
> cares of love, or love's affections.

In spite of the narrative and dramatic vigor of his verse, he interrupts his tale of martial deeds with interludes of gentle, pastoral scenes in accordance with the stylistic conventions of the time:

> . . . in a delightful
> spot chosen from many wooded fields,
> where the loveliest meadow is covered
> with an infinite number of flowers;
> there the trees stir with the susurro
> of a cool and tender breeze,
> and a gentle brook of calm and limpid water
> meanders through the grassy meadow.

What might be called the new poetry of the sixteenth century was formed by these elements of idyllic imagination, elegy, Petrarchian elegance, and of a revived Platonism so characteristic of the esthetics of the time. In the contemporary Hispanic world it was a style running counter to that of the old remnants of medieval poetry with its darker colors, starker realism, and greater popular and didactic vigor. This curious antithesis can be discerned as far away from Spain as Mexico only a few years after the Conquest. Pedro de Trejo, for example, who was born in Spain but went to the viceroyalty of Mexico at an early age, personifies the traditional verse of the fifteenth century, and in his *To Warn and Awaken Those Who Are Absorbed in Worldly Matters and Oblivious of God* he offers variations on the ancient theme so beautifully treated by Jorge Manrique:

> Awaken he who is asleep in the service of God
> and be alert.
> Be aware that he is lost
> for 'tis certain that God died for us.

And the young American-born Spaniard Francisco de Terrazas became an embodiment of the new lyric verse. This Mexican poet composed his *Sonnets about Flowers* in language that sought to emulate the aristocratic refinement of Garcilaso de la Vega. Pearls, "golden ringlets," the "warm, green spring," memories of serene days, and a mingling of a luminous tranquillity and a vague melancholy infuse his sonnets.

> Let go the golden ringlets of hair
> that hold my soul enmeshed,

and restore to the untrodden snow
its whiteness blended with those roses.

Two important figures of Spanish Petrarchism—Gutierre de Ce-
tina, the inspired writer of madrigals, and the prolific Juan de la
Cueva—lived in Mexico during the second half of the sixteenth
century; possibly their influence explains the touch of refinement and
elegance in Terraza's poetry. And, in line with this Italianate current, chronicles of adventures growing out of the Conquest were
composed in verse—for example, the voluminous *Pilgrim of the Indies,* by Antonio Saavedra Guzmán. There was no novel as such, for
which reason the expression of novelistic elements growing out of
the developing Creole or naturalized existence tended to gravitate
toward either the chronicle cultivated largely by clergymen after the
Conquest or bad imitations of Ercilla's epic which appeared throughout Spanish America. Among the latter were: *Antarctic Arms,* by
Miramontes y Zuazuola in Peru; *Elegies of Famous Men of the
Indies,* by Juan de Castellanos in New Granada (Colombia); *Arauco
Tamed*—the best sequel of *The Araucana*—by Pedro de Oña; *Untamed Purén,* by Álvarez de Toledo; and the *Wars of Chile,* by Juan
de Mendoza Monteagudo.

Contact with the New World began to put a distinctive stamp on
traditional forms of Spanish poetry: ballads, Christmas carols, and
medleys in honor of some saint. This is evident in the ingenuous
freshness of such poets as: Hernán González de Eslava, one of the
early creators of religious drama in New Spain; the Jesuit Pedro de
Hortigosa; and Rosas de Oquendo, the first to sing of the *mestizo*
elements. This new poetry helped to spread the Catholic faith by
supplying symbols comprehensible to the people, and also contribu-
ted to the new linguistic sensitivity that the Spanish language was
acquiring on the Mexican plateau, as is plainly seen in the work of
Rosas de Oquendo. Even poets of purely Spanish origin, such as
Juan de la Cueva and Eugenio de Salazar, had caught some of the
mysterious lure of the new words designating fruits, trees, and foods
in their songs to Mexico.

In this transition, as European literature began to absorb naturalized or mixed elements of expression, there occurred a phenomenon similar to what happened at the very beginning in architecture. If the working drawings or architectural plans brought from Spain had to be adhered to in building the early churches in the viceroyalties of Mexico and Peru, and if an architect—Francisco Becerra, for example—erected structures of the purest Spanish Renaissance style in Mexico City and Puebla and even in the Peruvian highlands to which his travels later took him, either the European style had changed when the religious influence spread from the many missions and the plentiful native labor supply was used, or environmental conditions compelled adaptations. What is most original in our culture since the sixteenth century derives from this intrusion of indigenous motifs and the outcropping of native elements.

THE PEDAGOGY OF PROSELYTING

A fine book yet to be written is one that would tell in detail the story of the three centuries of Spanish evangelistic work that began in Santo Domingo, spread to Mexico, Central America, the northern coast of South America and throughout that continent, and produced the interesting social utopia of the Jesuits in the forests of Paraguay as one of its last and ripest fruits. Like all history this era of proselyting had its lights and shadows. On one hand, there were the violent methods of more than one stupid Spanish rustic-turned-clergyman who wished to ram the Faith down the throats of the natives "by tying up the Indians with rope," or the harsh bishop of Oaxaca, Pedro Guzmán de Maraver, who urged that it "be beaten into them," as Friar Francisco Toral, bishop of Yucatán, indignantly wrote to Philip II. On the other hand, the noble reverse of this attitude was the model efforts of the first Franciscans in Mexico, including such fine personalities as Gante, Sahagún, Motolinía, and Vasco de Quiroga. They developed a methodology, a code of ethics, and even an economic system of evangelizing that, far more than as an intriguing bit of antiquarianism, would seem to merit study even now as a useful experiment or model for the still-unfinished task of incorporating the Indian into modern technological civilization. According to Father Mendieta, Motolinía's feat of almost becoming an Indian child and of learning to know the natives by playing with them largely explains the psychological acumen with which the great missionaries—chiefly early Franciscans—began their experiment. The difficulties of their task can readily be imagined: abolishing the ancient blood cult in Mexico, for example; learning the language of the vanquished; inculcating a Christian concept of life in such a warlike, caste-ridden people as the Aztec; overcoming the hostile mistrust of the Spaniards; puttings the arts and crafts of the defeated races to use in a new system; and searching for words and symbols in the aboriginal languages which would be useful in simplifying the complexities of Christian doctrine. In some tongues, particularly that of the wild Tarascan in Michoacán, there were absolutely no words to express such concepts as "soul," the "infinite," the "absolute," and the like. According to García Icazbalceta, the Franciscan Jacobo de Tastera was one of the first to work out a system of visual education which, by using Aztec hieroglyphs, made accessible to the Indians the more important matters of religious instruction. Directed by the friars, the Mexicans themselves painted these hieroglyphics, which sometimes carried figurative representations over into the most remarkable phonetic associations.

Thus, to memorize a paternoster in Latin, for example, the word *pater* was associated with the Mexican *pantli* (a kind of banner) and the word *Noster* with the India *nochtli* (a prickly pear or fig). A banner followed by a prickly pear were the hieroglyphic symbols that enabled an Indian to recall the first words of the Christian prayer. Again, images and metaphors were sought in the circumscribed world of the native to bring religious ideas nearer to his mentality. Since the aborigines had marveled at the horses of the conquistadors, attributing supernatural strength and courage to these beasts, the worship quickly developed of the Apostle Saint James—the holy horseman—who from the sixteenth century is represented in crude little statues decorated by the hand of natives or half castes. Equally popular from the outset was the cult of the Virgin Mary, whom the Indians associated with the mother-goddesses of their pagan religion.

One of the originators of this Christian-Indian pedagogy was the friar Pedro de Gante, whose remarkable Saint Francis College of Mexico was the first of the institutions founded in the sixteenth century for teaching and evangelistic work by the Franciscans and Dominicans. These included Santa Cruz de Tlaltelolco, San Juan de Letrán, and Santa María de Todos los Santos. The concept of a self-sufficient community, with work done in coöperation and services exchanged—the idea that the remarkable bishop Vasco de Quiroga would expand on a much larger scale—first appeared in Pedro de Gante's useful endeavor. He began the teaching of arts and crafts in the New World, and the result of his brilliant effort was the skilled workmanship that marked the effectiveness and beauty of Mexican craftsmanship above all others in Spanish America. To establish itself firmly, the new Faith required quarrymen and masons to erect the walls of the churches, carpenters to fashion the timberwork, image makers, painters, and even musicians and singers to brighten the religious ceremonies. All these were trained in the workshops of the indefatigable Pedro de Gante, who thus, through the teaching of a craft, redeemed the Indian from being a mere clod tilling the soil, to which status the military spirit of the Conquest and the economic organization of the *encomienda* all too willingly consigned him. An artisan class was thus formed which was less defenseless than the peasant serfs attached to the agricultural estates or forced to labor in the mines. As this kind of workman increased in technical proficiency and his standards of living improved, he began to cross the boundaries of race and to breach the harsh barriers of caste. The training schools preserved what might be called an aboriginal elite, and to some extent they prevented a completely proletarian status for all the conquered elements. Whereas Friar Pedro de Gante's workshops provided artisans and master craftsmen for private and public works in the sixteenth century, the classrooms of Santa Cruz de Tlaltelolco trained leaders and magistrates for the native towns, translators and interpreters, and even a famous writer—Fernando de Alva Ixlilxóchitl—who, with a strong Indian flavor, turned into Spanish the myths set forth in the ancient hieroglyphics and the words of old Aztec songs.

Pedro de Gante's method did not undertake to substitute European ways for native ones, but tried to absorb these within the needs and imperatives of a new culture. From the outset, as Manuel Toussaint has pointed out, such older Indian arts as flower mosaics arranged on a grass matting, which the Indians termed *petatl*—hence our word *petate*—served to represent Christian figures. And the exceedingly delicate feather mosaics shared a similar metamorphosis. In the colonial period this typical art of the Aztec inspired such beautiful creations as the shield in featherwork presented to Philip II, the famous Mexican miter preserved at the Escorial, and other liturgical banners and trappings. Many painters and decorators of mid-sixteenth-century Mexico trained in these missionary schools bore Indian names: Pedro Quauhtli, Miguel Texochicuic, Luis Xochitototl, Pedro Chacala, and others. Before 1555, according to Toussaint, one of these native artists, Marcos de Aquino—or, according to others, Marcos Cipac—painted the first canvas of our Lady of Guadalupe, the religious symbol of the hybrid Mexican soul.

HISTORICAL WRITINGS OF THE MISSIONARIES

Two extraordinarily valuable endeavors of a cultural nature grew out of the earnest and understanding work of great missionaries among the natives in the sixteenth century. One was the methodical description of Indian customs, languages, and rites in which the Spanish friars anticipated the beginnings of modern ethnology; they collected material that formed the basis of this science in the New World. The other was a dream of social reform, of bettering the lot of the Indians through missions that inspired some of the utopian experiments of the time. We approach closer to the spirit of the Indian in the pages of Motolinía, Sahagún, Acosta, Durán, and of their disciples Tezozomoc and Alva Ixlilxóchitl than we do in the hieroglyphics of archaeological remains. Friar Toribio de Benavente (Motolinía) has bequeathed us one of the most genuine and candid portraits of the vanquished race in his *History of the Indians of New Spain*. It grew out of his forty-four years of missionary work in Spanish America, during which he tramped over steep trails from Mexico to distant Nicaragua, tirelessly founded convents, and compiled catechisms, sermons, and manuals in Indian languages. He identified himself with the native race by changing his surname Benavente to Motolinía, the beautiful Tlascalan word for the virtue of poverty, and with fervent religious ardor he embraced the cause of the defenseless Indian against the excesses of the conquistador.

Friar Bernardino de Sahagún defines the scope of his purpose in his *General History Concerning Matters of New Spain* as "a seine to catch every word of the Nahuatl language with its proper and metaphorical meanings and all its modes of speech." The original plan of the work, which was considerably modified in the two versions— Indian and Spanish—that have come down to us, included a large-scale scheme of every aspect and characteristic of aboriginal society. The work was divided into four basic parts, designated by the author as: Gods, Heaven and Hell, Seigniory, and Human Matters. Many Indians collaborated by reporting fables, myths, and the intricacies of their social organization in a work that may be regarded as the richest storehouse of ethnological data ever assembled in Spanish America or, for that matter, anywhere. Two centuries and a half before Voltaire and Herder, Sahagún had a keen intuition about what was later called the "history of culture." No research on the Mexican Indians can be done without consulting this monumental work, which seems to grow fresher and more up-to-date with the progress of ethnology. It supplies archaeologists and ethnologists with analytical material enabling them better to understand what the early monuments, pictographs, and statues have to tell.

In contrast to the chronicles of the great military leaders or aristocratic observers of the Conquest, who invariably regarded the Indian with the dominating eye of a Spanish conqueror, the friar-historians, who were almost always at odds with these overlords, touched what might be called the inner life of the aborigines. The rigorous apprenticeship in native languages to which they subjected themselves, their living close to the Indians through long years, their necessary role in the early convents as protectors and counselors against the abuses of the conquistadors, their journeys on foot and remarkable adaptation to the American environment—all attest to the soundness of the historical writings of these missionaries. Few works have so authentic a ring as Father Diego Durán's curious *History of the Indians of New Spain,* the Spanish prose of which seems to have taken on some of the static or diffuse qualities of Aztec style. The sources of this work were the codices of hieroglyphics and the anonymous account of a Mexican Indian thinking in his own language. The narrative style of the author—a half-caste who became a friar—was so unlike any purely Western way of writing that its publisher in 1867 described the work as a "history basically Mexican with a Spanish physiognomy" and felt that it was his duty to "tidy it up" before publication to make it readable. The historical accounts of Alvarado Tezozomoc and Alva Ixlilxóchitl immerse us in a kind of psychological mystery as does the *New Chronicle and Good Guide,* a similar work of the Peruvian Huaman Poma de Ayala, written in the same period.

A truly exceptional work results when the aboriginal elements are perfectly fused with the most refined humanism of Europe, as in the *Royal Commentaries of the Incas* of the Inca Garcilaso de la Vega —the best of all the literature of the colonial period. In this work, history seems transformed into something more personal and exquisitely individualized such as an elegy or a poem. It is for this reason a unique piece of work, much more a product of art than of action or of a social attitude, as in the writings of Sahagún or Motolinía.

SOCIAL UTOPIAS

In sixteenth-century Mexico, social utopias—the dream of a better world and the rule of justice—found a matchless interpreter and practitioner in Vasco de Quiroga, a judge of the Audiencia later elevated to the rank of Bishop of Michoacán. Recent studies emphasize the influence of Sir Thomas More's famous work and the social thought of the Renaissance in general on Vasco de Quiroga's history-making effort. The distinguished Mexican historian Silvio Zavala has published a facsimile copy of the Frobenus (Basel, 1518) edition of the *Utopia,* with reproductions of manuscript notes of Bishop Zumárraga, friend and confidant of the Michoacán reformer. A scrutiny of details in Quiroga's writings—such as the *Ordinances* of his towns and hospitals, his *Plan* for agricultural settlements sent to the Council of the Indies, and his *Will and Testament* of 1565—testifies to the wise and profound social awareness that undergirded his reforming activities. Indeed, the Platonic dream—now impregnated with Christian fervor—of a more harmonious world order had revived in the hearts of the missionary humanists. Could any passage be more revealing of their Christianized Platonism than the interesting prologue of Bishop Zumárraga's *Christian Rule*, published in 1547:

> One of the signs to determine whether something is truly of God and created by His divine hand, the Apostle Saint Paul teaches, is its order and law, for everything that God creates has order and law to which it adheres by nature. The heavens show it in their cyclic movements of day and night. In no less fashion the elements, plants, animals, and birds reveal it to us, for they have not maliciously destroyed the law and order that God created for them. Only wretched man wanders outside of the law, thus offending God and his blessed Maker.

A figure of high caliber—Vasco de Quiroga—started the first great utopia in the New World to create a human order bordering on divine harmony. In the sunlit land of Michoacán, where Quiroga pacified the warlike Indians in the days of the Conquest, the memory survives to this day of the remarkable experiments in collective work farms, hospitals and asylums, public granaries and warehouses, work schedules varied by exercise and recreation, and small home crafts. Alfonso Reyes has written some charming pages in his *Ultima Thule* (published in Mexico in 1942), on the fair-minded, humanitarian, and poetic scope of such a noble effort to civilize a people. Europe's fruits—its abundant garden products, domestic looms to spin wool, flax, cotton, and silk, and even its popular arts and festivals—all flourished in this temporal Arcadia planned and directed by Quiroga in which a wise and ingenious coördination of economic activities placed a single craft in each community. By avoiding overproduction, this arrangement maintained a balanced and advantageous exchange of goods between the various towns and villages. For instance, Cepula had woodcutting as its chief industry; Teremendo manufactured footwear for the villages of Michoacán; Uruapan produced lacquer ware, still one of the most attractive products of popular Mexican art. Vasco de Quiroga's utopia was reborn in 1606 when the Jesuits established their first great missions on the Paraguay river, fenced off meadows for communal cattle, set up workshops and rudimentary trade schools, and brought roving Indians closer to the peaceful, workaday life of settlements. For a century and a half (1606–1767) Paraguay—with forests of *ceibo* trees and orange groves along its large rivers, altars and church roofs made of American mahogany—would be a land of utopian fancy. Here war and economic discord were abolished, and here—as in Lucian's dream, which Vasco de Quiroga recalled now and then—the golden age had returned, those allegedly happier, more tranquil days of the world. But this drive for social reform slowed with the creeping languor of the Spanish state and its bureaucratic red tape, which let these humanitarian exploits of the early missionaries wither on the vine. In the seventeenth century—the so-called baroque age—most clergymen displayed a preference for wealthy convents in the viceregal capitals, and a liturgical splendor replaced creative faith. The empty pomp of the baroque was substituted for the reality of indigenous rural life in Spanish America which Quiroga and Pedro de Gante had known how to assess.

During the first century of the Conquest the churches and monasteries were spiritual battle grounds for the exhausting task of proselyting. They were also the places where native languages were learned, where the community's economic needs were met, and they even served as a defense against hostile Indians. In these harsh conditions even the imported art of Spain tended to revert to more medieval and archaic forms. Like rude fortresses bristling with battlements, whose whitewashed spires framed the blue of the sky, the early Franciscan churches stood on the Mexican plateau at Huejotzingo, Cholula, and Tlalmanalco. Indian labor, which was extensively used in construction work, often adorned the Spanish-type walls with stylized designs of flowers, feathers, birds, and geometrical figures similar to those in their ancient codices—the anthropomorphic and naturalistic themes of European iconography mingled with Aztec hieroglyphics. A similar phenomenon was noted in Peruvian architecture. As the Church grew wealthier, styles were more and more embellished until, in the last third of the sixteenth century, buildings of plateresque elegance were created displaying such exquisite gold and silver work as that adorning the façade of the church at Acolman. In the seventeenth century this refinement reached a high point in the lush intricacy of the baroque, which assumed an Oriental splendor in the bright light of Mexico; surfaces were inlaid with tiles and multicolored traceries in Arabic fashion, and shimmering altarpieces were made of New World species of wood carved and coated with firelike gilt.

Although the Church lost something of its early proselyting zeal on passing from the century of Conquest into the baroque era, nevertheless through its liturgy and art it spoke a language that was most comprehensible to the mass of the Indians.

FIESTAS, THEATER, AND OTHER MESTIZO FORMS OF EXPRESSION

Already in the sixteenth century the religious festivals were the clearest and most colorful symbol of the interrelation of the Spaniard and the native. Incorporated into Catholic practices were the dances, pantomimes, masquerades, or ceremonies that to this day attend the celebration of traditional Spanish holy days—the Corpus Christi, the Magi Kings, Our Lady of Candelaria, or Saint John the Baptist —by the mixed populations of South America; these forms of observance speak more truly to the Indians' condition than do the purely European ritual. There are communities and regions where more than one rite is still preserved undiluted by Western influences. In an interesting interpretive essay the Mexican ethnologist Manuel Gamio describes a ceremony honoring the "stag god" in which villages of Zongolica in the state of Veracruz invoke rain and good harvests by building huge bonfires. Birds are then sacrificed and grains of cereal burned while a venerable Indian, the guardian of these strange, incomprehensible rituals, entreats his god in archaic words of his own language. Gamio also notes how an ancient symbolism still hovers over other Mexican festivals. The dances to the Virgin de la Soledad retain motifs used in the worship of Huitzilopochtli, and anyone watching the dance groups in the popular ceremonies at Guadalupe, Remedios, and Tacuba can easily imagine that similar garbs and pantomimes conspicuously displayed their striking colors and rhythms in the Aztec temples.

A similar process of adaptation or assimilation of Indian and Catholic elements occurred throughout Spanish America and even among the most backward tribes, such as the Araucanians in Chile. In central Chile, where the Indians were more readily subjugated and Christianized, the raucous *guilatún* was transformed into the curious festival of "running to Christ." The Araucanians still celebrate it with much wild shouting and running about as a means of petitioning their *pillán* to send rain. Featured by gay calvacades of mounted peasants, pursued by obstreperous bands of boys, this fiesta is held in many rural villages and even on the outskirts of Santiago, the capital. In Bolivia and the Peruvian highlands, as Uriel García has pointed out, religious festivals such as the "Lord of Earthquakes," Copacabana, Apostle Saint James, Santa Rosa, and the splendid Corpus Christi take on a most extraordinary variety of features.

The earliest indications of drama appear in the sixteenth century as an adjunct of religious processions. It is a theater in the native tongue like the one attempted in Mexico in 1553 by Friar Andrés de Olmos, author of an *Allegory of the Last Judgment*, performed at the Colegio de Santiago de Tlaltelolco. And there were many others staged in church yards, public squares, and convent patios. A famous one at Tlascala in 1549 assembled more than a thousand Indians in a single performance. Cuzco witnessed a considerable development of this kind of drama in the seventeenth century. The theater in the Spanish language began to be naturalized by absorbing local words and expressions; usually the genres were morality plays or colloquies and the short skit. Since the Mexicans and Peruvians were both familiar with the theater through staging many of their own civic and religious ceremonies, this kind of propaganda in behalf of the new

Faith proved acceptable and comprehensible. In pre-Hispanic Peru, according to the Inca Garcilaso de la Vega, there had been two kinds of plays: one was inspired by military feats, battles, and victories of the Incas and was strictly aristocratic, whereas the other made use of domestic themes taken from "agriculture, household matters, and family life." Some of the more symbolic plays readily lent themselves to evangelistic drama. The festival of Saint John the Baptist explained the sacrament of baptism simply and encouraged the Indians to receive it. A series of morality plays—*The Fall of the First Parents, The Annunciation of the Nativity of Saint John, The Annunciation of Our Lady,* and *The Nativity of Saint John the Baptist*—provided a lively reconstruction of the theological history of man until his redemption by the coming of Christ and the institution of the first Christian sacrament. The Corpus Christi popularized the mystery of the Eucharist, and the representation of All Saints Day symbolized the Church triumphant. The Gospel theme was adapted locally by having the Indians themselves march in the parade of the Magi Kings along with the shepherds and their servants who came with offerings. In Cuzco—where the seventeenth-century native theater achieved almost greater importance than it did in Mexico—several delightful works were written, such as the morality plays *Usca Paukar, Yauri Tito Inca,* and particularly *The Prodigal Son.* Most impressive evidence of interest in drama in the Quechua language appeared later in a play called *Ollantay,* the author and exact date of which are unknown. Recent criticism places its composition in the second half of the seventeenth century or in the early eighteenth. With its romantic theme curiously reminiscent of the Spanish legend of *The Sweethearts of Teruel, Ollantay* offers a pleasing picture of life in Cuzco. This serious play remains one of the unsolved literary and linguistic problems of our cultural history. It was possibly written by a learned *mestizo* who, while well acquainted with the language, feeling, and fables of his Indian countrymen, was apparently not entirely unaware of the techniques and resources of the Western theater.

The Prodigal Son, whose author was presumedly the celebrated *mestizo* of Cuzco, Espinosa Medrano, impresses me as the masterpiece of the indigenous theater of Spanish America. If Espinosa Medrano did write it in the seventeenth century, we have another interesting literary puzzle. Although this writer—a thoroughgoing champion of the artificialities of Gongorism—had composed an *Apology for Góngora* in the most complicated of baroque prose, in the work written in Quechua he is a poet of limpid simplicity who knows how to peer directly into the Indians' world and describe it in concise, beautifully chiseled verse. The Biblical legend is transferred to the lofty heights of the Andes; and in a scene of lively realism the Indian eats his "potatoes from Laikakota and Pacus, his corn from Potosí, and his mushrooms from Condoroma." Of extraordinary beauty is the scene in which the young sinner is tempted by the courtesan Aicha:

> Thou still dost not recognize me? I am the great and powerful Queen Aicha—the loveliest and most sought-after Aicha. The mighty and the strong likewise fear woman. She subdues them all, from the lowliest shepherd to the loftiest monarch. Gentlemen of every sort follow trembling in my wake. Wherever I do go they but look into my countenance and are reflected in my eyes. I tread upon golden diadems. Men's faces are my sandals. I despise him who pursues me; the bold and arrogant win me; who flees from me, him I ultimately follow and seek. If my lover burns with passion, I am cold; if he cools, then I begin to burn. A breeze becomes a tempest. My heart is forever restless. Each day I arise to a new lover. If the mood strikes me I abandon the one who loves me, the one who expected that very day to lie upon my bosom. By all men am I indulged, beloved, and sought after.

The play closes with a tender dialogue between Kuyaj Yaya, the old Indian father—symbol of providence and heavenly love—and his eldest son Hanan Saga, who reproaches him for the affection with which he greets the returning prodigal:

> What does this mean? Why is it, sir, that thou welcomest back such a libertine son who abandoned his father and squandered all that thou gavest him? Thou hast favored him and arrayed him in fine raiment and, besides, thou hast killed the fatted pig. But for me who has honored his father, who has always

stayed at thy side taking care of thee, never hast thou done as
much for me. Not even a llama hast thou offered me. Never hast
thou said unto me: "Here, eat with thy friends, with the companions of thy youth."

And Kuyaj Yaya answers:

My son, thou art ever with me, and all that I have is thine.
When thy brother returned, however, I had found again one
who was lost and as if dead. That was why I was so happy. Thee
I shall love and esteem as much and always.

A truly naturalized theater took root through the lively and popular tradition of the religious play and the short skit. Drama in Spanish also began in the sixteenth century, but its symbols usually derived from Mexican words and figures of speech as in the *Colloquies*
of the presbyter Juan Pérez Ramírez, and still more delightfully in
the spontaneous and graceful art of Hernán González Eslava. The
latter at times achieves the freshness and lyric simplicity of a Gil
Vicente in the Christmas carols and short songs intercalated in his
Colloquies. The pastoral symbol or shepherd type so common in the
Italianate literature of the time is used in his work in its simplest
and most popular form:

> Didst see, Pascual, a little child
> in a ruined doorway?
> I saw him and I am enchanted
> by such a sweet little shepherd lad.
> Though dressed in rags,
> what didst thou think of the lad?
> Why, that surely he is the head shepherd
> of the heavenly flocks.

The old Spanish game of riddles and medleys, whose wit depends
upon puns, off-hand metaphors, or associating unlike things, was
useful for the poet's ingenuous presentation of religious ideas:

> What is it that is,
> that strikes you and you do not see it?
> It is the wind;

it is God in the Sacrament
that your eyes do not see,
but you will see it through Faith
and through sound understanding.

Elsewhere gamblers—with salty, picaresque names such as John
Pothook and Lope Smalloaf—argue in raucous and very colloquial
Spanish in a Mexican dive or, while Saint Gregory, Saint Jerome,
and Saint Augustine are discussing profound theological questions,
they denounce Lucifer with insults phrased in choice terms of earthy
pungency:

Let the old he-goat bully
suffer forever;
I vow that, if the old scoundrel
should come along this way,
'pon my word, I'd lick him
and tar him with bacon grease.

Oh, to hell with the filthy
old Cerberus!
Angina in his gullet!
Angina and bad tumors to him!
Let him pump bellows
in a blacksmith's shop on Tacuba street.

Would to the true God the Devil
had an arm in Coyoacán
his legs in Oaxaca,
his top in Cuernavaca
and his belly in Michoacán!

May a foul cancer afflict
the old he-whore,
and all kinds of tumors!
And may he get bad pains in his side,

and his tongue be yanked out
from the very nape of his neck!

In an interesting study Francisco de Icaza discussed a writer of short skits, the first dramatist of this genre in the Indies, Cristóbal de Llerena, who, about 1548, composed colorful dialogues on the island of Santo Domingo in which he mingled humanistic inventiveness with popular satire. In one of his skits, which caused his expulsion from the island on the complaint of local judges and by royal indictment, there appears what nowadays we would call the beginning of "social criticism." The skit is a protest of the common people and the embryonic middle class against abuses of authority by scribes and lawyers who apply the law in their own way, by unscrupulous merchants who take advantage of the currency shortage to overcharge for their goods, and by speculators who sell provisions to the ships of the annual fleet and thereby raise prices in the local market. In this discussion of the rich man's and the poor man's rights Llerena places his engaging talent on the side of the unprotected. After this early nonconformist returned to Spain, he vanished without a trace, according to the documents examined by Icaza.

The free spirit and the adventurous, creative zeal to invent new ways and to understand the aboriginal way of life characteristic of the sixteenth century had withered away by the seventeenth century: a static, indolent period followed a dynamic one. As we shall see, beginning with Philip II the Indies suffered the same tragic deterioration as Spain. The great days of the Conquest had ended and the Spanish nation moved into an inglorious epoch of trying to hold what it had acquired and to live in isolation, stubbornly resisting the new cultural tendencies developing in the rest of Europe.

The Coming of the
Seventeenth Century

SPANISH DECADENCE REFLECTED IN THE INDIES

In the closing stanzas of his vast, versified chronicle *Elegies of Famous Men of the Indies* (1589)—written at Tunja, a city of the New Kingdom of Granada (Colombia)—Juan de Castellanos, then advanced in years, sadly remarked that a new generation preferring enjoyment to fighting had taken the place of the hardy men of the Conquest of America. Flocking to the cities founded by the Spaniards in the highlands of the Andes and on the warm shores of the Caribbean during a century of stirring history now came crowds of young people from Spain wholly indifferent to the counsels of the brave and seasoned veterans who had won their places the hard way. These sturdy men of action saw themselves supplanted by civilian officials who had merely come "to stuff themselves," to use Bishop Zumárraga's vigorous expression. And there is confirmatory evidence in the extraordinary letter of Lope de Aguirre, "the Tyrant of the Andes," to Philip II, which was a flaming challenge to Spain. If we disregard its pathological elements of rancor, this communication reveals the attitude, though greatly exaggerated, of the soldier, adventurer, and conquering veteran toward Spanish administrators and the lettered class. Juan de Castellanos was acquainted with every variety of experience that the sixteenth-century conquest had offered; he had been an adolescent soldier in the Antilles, a trader on the Isle of Pearls (Margarita), a settler at Coro and Cubagua, and a traveler over the rough trails from Cartagena on the coast to Popoyán high in the Andes. Later in life he became a clergyman and was the first parish priest at Tunja situated in the legend-haunted country of the Zipa Indians. In bringing his long narrative to a close he noted that everything was changing and that, among the new social values, the courage and imagination of the earlier days no longer counted. He wished to evoke the memory of the men of fame he had known in the Antilles, in northern South America, and in New Granada because they had all vanished. From the vantage point of his eighty adventurous years the old, free-lance fighter of the Conquest reminds the vain and conceited men who now had come to exploit America that:

> War equipment and numbers are wont to be useless
> when the wise counsels are missing
> that grey hairs customarily provide the callow.

These last survivors of the great century thus give the impression that the truly epic times were over and that a sedentary, static present had begun to eclipse a heroic, creative past. But, after all, this is merely a reflection of the history of the mother country where Spain, beginning with the reign of Philip II, was obviously declining. Having launched the last Crusade at the beginning of the modern age, and having conquered the New World while striving at the same time to realize the impossible dream of Catholic unity by subduing Europe, the Hispanic world could no longer spend its strength but had to husband it. The defeat of the Spanish Armada in the storm-ridden North Sea was truly of symbolic significance. By then the commercial exploits of the English, the middle-class culture of Protestant countries, the well-defined absolutism of the French state, and the growth of natural sciences and technology were reducing to an anachronism the militant religious ideal so long held by the Spaniard. All these historical trends were directly opposed to what Spain had defended with such stubborn faith and tenacity. Miguel de Cervantes, writing his *Don Quixote* in the early years of the seventeenth century, would finally cause the world of knight errantry to totter and fall. Spanish pride—the pride of a people once the greatest power in sixteenth-century Europe, the *nazione armígera,* as the Italians expressively put it—now not only sealed itself off from the new trends of history but even launched a rash and hopeless attack against them.

History, outside of the early annals of China, has possibly never recorded a more determined and fanatic defensive policy than that of Spain under Philip II. In the European community of nations Spain truly became an anachronism. When we read the seventeenth-century accounts of travel in Spain written by Frenchmen or Italians —Madam D'Aulnoy's readable book, for example—we realize how exotic and, at times, incomprehensible Spanish ways had become to other Western peoples. The keen logic and careful analytical habits of the French and the practical, mundane empiricism of the English are meaningless in this slightly fanciful world which rears its laby-rinthian structure of theology heavenward. Elsewhere in Europe the "kingdom of man" had begun, but Spain still stood for the "kingdom of God."

How did this decadence, this stubborn defensive attitude of Spain affect the distant Indies? Without digging into the well-known sub-ject of Spain's plight under the Habsburgs, we may look for the American aspects of the problem within its own seventeenth- and eighteenth-century society.

SEVENTEENTH CENTURY SOCIETY

A few chronicles of colonial cities, such as the interesting *Annals of Potosí* by Martínez Vela, dealing with Potosí, or the *Lima Diary* of Mugaburu, enable us, as no other documents do, to peer into the mysteries and details of the torpid life of these communities, includ-ing their social and economic practices and their all-pervading religi-osity. Bishop Lizárraga, Friar Antonio de la Calancha, and others have created for us in ornate prose a picture of our seventeenth-century cities; and in the Inquisition proceedings, collected by José T. Medina in Peru and Chile and by Genaro García in Mexico, the sociologist and cultural historian can learn about the preoccupations, prejudices, and trivialities of that colonial world proudly aware of its differentness. The first contrast between the adventurous, warlike days of the Conquest and the long noonday nap which our seventeenth and early eighteenth centuries resemble, is an economic one. With the Indians subdued, the semifeudal *encomienda* grants distributed (many being reapportioned, however, in the course of the seventeenth century), and the forced service of the *mita* providing cheap labor in Guanajuato and Zacatecas in Mexico and Huancavalica and Potosí in Peru, the Spanish upper class, mostly descendants of the conquistadors, along with the Church made wealthy by legacies and gifts, entered upon the fullest enjoyment of the benefits of the land.

As so often stated, life in the English colonies of North America presented a sharp contrast because no plentiful supply of native labor was available nor precious metal to exploit. Consequently, a small farm economy developed in the wet, forest-covered lands of New England. On the other hand, colonial society in Spanish America during its seventeenth and a large part of the eighteenth centuries was aristocratic and, viewing manual labor with disdain, thrust this obligation upon a swarm of Negroes, Indians, and mixed elements. Very different from the pomp and ceremony of a Spanish colonial city was the mode of life in a tiny Puritan village of New England. The small, wooden houses of the latter, its strong coöperative spirit, its rural psychology, its ethical concepts derived from the Old Testament, and the poverty of its church whose pastor received compensation in the form of firewood for his hearth or food for his larder when his flock was unable to pay a salary in money, all indicated a total dissimilarity. In contrast to this frugality, Bishop Lizárraga in Lima assailed luxury. There, according to this chronicler's engaging description, a lady's outfit consisted of cork-soled slippers with buckles and decorated with designs of half moons, rosettes, chains, and golden necklaces; bracelets; gold bodkins to fasten her hair; earrings, perfumes, rings, and precious stones. Martínez Vela in his *Annals* telling the story of the greatness of that mining center from the middle of the seventeenth century—when its population of 170,000 made it the most populous city in the Spanish domains—to its decline in the silver crisis of the eighteenth century which reduced it to the modest size of a provincial town, dwells at length on its prodigal and vainglorious society. Martínez frequently describes the medieval jousts with reed lances, the celebrated "Joust of the Ring" with horsemen displaying their gaily caparisoned steeds, mansions richly furnished with rugs and carpeting, Asiatic lacquer work, ivory, and porcelains brought in the Manila galleons to Mexico and transshipped to Peru, and weddings and baptismal ceremonies in which families competed in lavish expenditures.

With the forced labor of the Indians and, therefore, without any incentive or need for technological improvements American-born Spaniards found life in general easy in the Indies. Father Calancha compared the abundance of the New World in his *Chronicle* with the austerity and poverty of Spain. "Here the most commonplace person has his soup the year around while in Spain only the wealthy have it, and here the plebeian eats more in a week than the most fortunate do there in a month." The Indies were still a land of plenty because there was no overpopulation and everything grew freely. In Peru "there are fowls like flowers," in Tucumán "a cow is worth a peso, in Paraguay half a peso, and about the same in Chile." "Three-year-old muttons go for five or six reales."

As the sixteenth century merged into the seventeenth, the Church likewise grew more sedentary and fond of luxury. It was more interested in dominating the Creole society of Spanish Americans than in harvesting Indian souls. To gain this control, Franciscans were at odds with Dominicans, Dominicans with Jesuits in the colonial universities, monks with secular clergymen in the bishoprics, and the Church in general with the state. These conflicts mainly took the form of petty feuds over matters of jurisdiction and ceremonial etiquette. Immense wealth became unproductive as it flowed into the coffers of the religious orders and of the dioceses from the tithes and first fruits, from contributions of the crown and of feudal overlords, from dowries of nuns and friars on entering convents and monasteries, from legacies and bequests, and from parish fees that were much higher than in Spain. All this income and property were held in mortmain and hence inalienable. According to the conservative estimate of Lucas Alamán, by the end of the colonial period at least half of all property, urban and rural, in the viceroyalty of Mexico alone was thus controlled.

The church-fortress, or evangelistic training center, of the early missionaries evolved into the elaborately ornate baroque structures of Spanish Creole architecture, and most of the intrigues in colonial cities emanated from the locutories of sumptuous convents. Every viceroy and bishop was threatened by monkish uprisings as, for example, when Bishop Palafox was forced to resign in Mexico after long-drawn-out litigation with all civil and ecclesiastical authorities and including appeals to the pope and the king; or again when an ignorant and fanatic mob was incited against the viceroy Carillo de Mendoza and began to set fire to the viceregal palace, shouting "Lutheran" and "heretic." The medieval quarrels between Church and state crossed to America to become even more puerile there. Since it was inexpedient to attack royal patronage, that is, the control of the Church granted by the popes to the Spanish kings, conflict arose over simple matters of hierarchy and jurisdiction. Whenever the inquisitors visited the viceroy, for example, an exact record had to be made of his manner in receiving them—whether he was standing or seated, and what were the ceremonial acts or courtesies that one party extended to the other. Any formula of politeness considered inadequate to the occasion was immediately subject to the most distorted interpretation as is indicated in the curious set of documents compiled by Genaro García. A mere lack of formality might stir up a controversy that could reach even the ears of the king who acted as a mediator and arbitrator in matters of petty gossip through his royal decrees. He had to decide on the seating order at the observance of Holy Thursday, which authority was entitled to the key to the tabernacle, and other trivial matters of protocol. In the administrative language of the time Spain seemed like a mandarin government that gave all its attention to the properly chosen rite, to the excessively ceremonious formula, and to subtle interpretation of the intrigues of any official, which became a public problem; and a parasitic superstructure of colonial functionaries, clergymen, and lords of entailed estates rested upon a vast pedestal of servile classes.

An aristocratic society, clearly solidified by the seventeenth century,

accentuated social distinctions and class prejudices. Although miscegenation still continued somewhat beyond the pale of the law and
the ordinances, a more jaundiced racial attitude had supplanted the
freedom of earlier days when the Spaniards contracted morganatic
unions with Indian women and fathered a select company of half-
castes to which Inca Garcilaso de la Vega or Alva Ixlilxóchitl belonged. But prejudice in the Spanish colonies stemmed from political
and economic causes rather than from a sexual attitude or an ethical
taboo as in the English settlements of North America. This situation
in Hispanic America was a reflection of the dream of religious and
ethnic unity that began with the Catholic Monarchs Ferdinand and
Isabella in Spain, and reached a climax in the explusion of the Moors
under Philip III. From the fervor of the Counter Reformation grew
a mistrust of the "New Christians," which ultimately resulted in the
demand of proof of "clean blood" as a social requirement.

Useless and petty sumptuary laws like those prescribing the clothes
and ornaments that could be worn and those forbidden to the
"castes," doubtless played their part in inflaming the bitter hatreds
that in 1609 had already caused Negro riots in Mexico. These dis-
turbances and the dangerous uprising of the Mexican masses in 1692
were the prelude of the widespread upheavals that, toward the end
of the next century, afflicted Spanish America in the highlands of
Peru, in Paraguay, and in New Granada. Designations, either colorful
or derogatory, to define the degree of racial mixture—mulatto, Moor,
salta atrás (backslider), *lobo* (wolf), *albarazado, cambujo* (brawny
mule), *zambaigo* or *zambo* (offspring of Negro and Indian), *tente
en el aire* (offspring of quadroon and mulatto), and the like—all
helped to maintain sullen resentment and a sense of ethnic inferiority. When the lush artificiality of the baroque gave way to a more
forthright style of writing, the latter exuded a cold, ironic rancor,
evident, for example, in the curious eighteenth-century work *Guide
of Blind Travelers*, allegedly written by a *mestizo* under the pen
name "Concolorcorvo."

THE INQUISITION AND THE SPIRIT OF THE
COUNTER REFORMATION

The Inquisition, like no other institution, exemplifies the defensive
character of seventeenth-century colonial culture, its narrowness and
spiritual sterility. Though Zumárraga and the early bishops, as well
as Franciscan and Dominican friars, exercised authority as deputies
and officials of the Spanish Inquisition and the first *autos de fé* took
place between 1536 and 1570, the Holy Office was not an integral
part of life in the Indies until near the end of the sixteenth century
when it was formally established in Lima (1570) and Mexico City
(1571). From then on this tribunal acted as a superorganism whose
intrusive and vaguely delimited powers alarmed both the civil and
ecclesiastical authorities. Many a viceroy feared the inquisitors and
tried to pursue a prudent and ingratiating policy in their presence.
The undefined scope of the legal functions of the Holy Office, the
fact that its decisions were not subject to appeal, and the unquestion-
ing obedience and coöperation that it demanded as the "secular arm"
of the Church, all constituted an invitation to abuse. Such abuse
included both the fanatical type of justice entrusted to the Church
and the perquisites and privileges that the Inquisition enjoyed in administering seized properties and the monetary gains which it sometimes derived from illicit trafficking. As early as 1605 the king wrote
to the Mexican inquisitors stating that he had heard that several
of them, especially the treasurer, had suddenly become very rich and
"owned large estates and sheep and cattle ranches."

An inspection of the Lima tribunal in the eighteenth century
touched off a big scandal in 1746 and exposed the vast dealings in
contraband of two inquisitors of that city, Calderón and Unda, along
with their luxurious habits and their hardly canonical mode of life.
It is understandable that such an institution, working in secret and
accepting mere accusation as valid evidence, would become a dangerous and, at times, corrupt public organism. Enjoying autonomous
status with respect to the bishops, royal courts, and civil government,
it could sequestrate properties and thus bring huge sums into its

coffers. In his *History of Heterodoxy*, Menéndez y Pelayo defended the Inquisition as a necessary instrument of religious unity without which the sixteenth-century wars of religion would have drenched Spain in blood. But, even accepting the eminent Spanish critic's highly conservative point of view, a serious charge can be brought against the Inquisition in the Indies in that it did not have to deal with any important matters of dogma. Heresy was almost unknown in the colonies, and the most important indication of freedom of thought traceable in our sixteenth- and seventeenth-century culture was a faint tinge of Erasmus's ideas limited to a small group of scholars. Moreover, until the time of the Council of Trent, Erasmian thought was not definitely banned by the Church. The Inquisition must be censured for its childish and stupid attitude, its total lack of feeling or understanding in dealing with a complex Indo-Spanish society, as well as for its torture racks and lugubrious secret chambers that were the common denominators, according to Menéndez y Pelayo, of the horrible penal systems in Europe at that time. The psychological sensitivity and sympathetic understanding of the Indians that we saw in the sixteenth-century missionaries apparently disappeared altogether, and the grim inquisitors of the following century, ever on the lookout for guilt and evidences of sin, bent every effort, with sadistic delight, to ferret them out.

From another point of view the Inquisition often seemed a clearing house of the tidbits of gossip on private lives in the viceregal capitals, gleaned from dining rooms, kitchens, and bedrooms. Lawsuits which it instituted in Mexico and Peru are recorded in the excellent compilations of Medina and Genaro García. They tend to fall into four classes:

First, suits affecting the Judaizers, or those practicing Jewish rites, who claimed attention not only because of the need for religious unity, but because their talent for business management had made them owners of the best commercial houses in Lima in the second half of the seventeenth century and successful entrepreneurs in Mexico's rich mining centers. As the trial proceedings in 1648 against the wealthy Martín Treviño family in New Spain amply testify, the persecution of the Jews did not spare even thirteen- or fourteen-year-old boys and girls. If pork had not been eaten on a given day, or if a bedroom had been brightened up and bedclothes changed on Friday, such acts, in the absence of better evidence, were sufficient "proof" of Judaism.

Second, criminal proceedings against the few English and Dutch Protestants who were captured when pirate expeditions were broken up, or who had slipped into the country and formed part of its invariably cosmopolitan population of the mining towns in Mexico and Peru. The first to be burned at the stake in Lima was a Fleming, Juan Millar, who perished in a Counter Reformation bonfire in 1548 well before the formal establishment of the Inquisition. A curious account of this crime of Lutheran heresy, as the inquisitors chose to call it, is set forth in an interesting pamphlet by Benjamín Vicuña Mackena entitled *Francisco Moyen, or the Inquisition in America.*

Third, since Protestants and Judaizers were sometimes in short supply, the Inquisition's jails were mostly stocked with native victims. The latter included Spaniards or Spanish Americans who exploited the credulity of villagers by donning the priest's cassock; now and then an injudicious curate let his instincts run wild in native communities; or religious charlatans, female and male, with a half-baked knowledge of mysticism and a familiarity with superstitious notions current in primitive areas, attracted a large following and acquired a specious aura of sanctity. Such, for example, were Ángela Carranza, famous in Córdoba (Argentina), and Francisco Ulloa in Santiago de Chile. Many Inquisition cases were directed against poor Negroes accused of blasphemy. When, as domestic servants, they were flogged by their masters, they sometimes sought to alleviate the agony by uttering anguished interjections in Castilian, "cursing God and His saints." Offenses of this sort were punished by appearing in public, a candle in hand, a rope about the neck, and a gag or muzzle, to make a recantation and to receive two hundred lashes.

Fourth, the Inquisition would busy itself with trivial matters such as that of a Negro slave girl who "talked from her chest." This possibly ventriloquist trick led many to think that it was an antic of the Devil. The investigation covered reams of paper with a jargonized prose after which the slave's owners were sentenced to sell her and to dispose of her within a stipulated number of days far beyond the limits of Mexico City. A familiar figure in the Inquisition records was the Devil who had grown more devilish in the American environment owing to what he had learned in his dealings with Indians and Negroes. Unlike Dr. Faustus, the humble half-caste or offspring of an Indian and a Negro did not need the Devil to propound a metaphysical problem or to ask for the boon of eternal youth. Rather, his need of Satanic intervention was for more tangible and concrete things. There was the instance of Francisco Rodríguez, a *zambo* or Indian-Negro mixture, "forty-three years old, occupation coachman and herdsman," who accused himself, in proceedings dated April 6, 1646, "of having had a pact with the Devil, paid him homage, and deeded himself as a slave for nine years at the expiration of which his Satanic majesty would carry him off to Hell." According to the inquisitors' report, the benefit to be derived from this supernatural deal (as witness whereof the Devil had offered Rodríguez a likeness of himself printed on a piece of parchment) was the gift of

> being able to fight off a thousand men, have any woman he liked, however high her rank and class, fight bulls or ride horses with no personal danger, journey back and forth to this city and elsewhere in a single night, however far away he might be, and many other fearful and dreadful things much too outrageous and offensive for proper Catholic ears.

The penalty imposed by the Inquisition upon Rodríguez, who today would have been promptly packed off to a sanitarium, was that he should display himself as a penitent with "a green candle in his hands, a rope around his neck, a white carapace, make a public recantation, receive two hundred lashes" and a knowledge of hell in life rowing as a galley slave.

The many sorcerers, male and female, brought to trial, both in Mexico and Peru, provide ethnologists with an engaging study. Besides the superstitions imported from Europe along with the age-old fear of witches that begot the many, cruel tales of witchcraft in Massachusetts among the Puritans, the presence of Indians and Negroes in our colonial society added mixed elements to these notions. Frequently, it seems, the humbled Indian or Negro, trying to make his own myths and practices mesh with the religion the Spaniards had taught him, saw in sorcery a kind of self-protection or something that somehow endowed his person with a mysterious authority. Even Spanish families that had migrated to the newer cities of Spanish America were subtly attracted by this weird and eerie underworld on coming in contact with servants of Negro or mixed blood. In this respect no story is so tragic and revealing as the one about Catalina de los Ríos y Lisperguer, a famous Chilean woman of the seventeenth century and a semifeudal *encomendera*, nicknamed *la Quintrala*, whose shocking biography, a mixture of lewdness and superstition, Benjamín Vicuña Mackena has pieced together in an excellent narrative. This is the other side of the coin, the gloomy side of the colonial life that Ricardo Palma depicts in his *Peruvian Traditions* as placid, picaresque, and colorfully ceremonious; it is the dark aspect of our early history whose prevailing ignorance and sense of repression demanded such unwonted outlets. The Potosí chronicle of Martínez Vela records sordid crimes with strong sexual overtones and shot through with elements of witchcraft and the black arts. Notwithstanding the apparently sound structure of the Catholic religion and morality brought by the Spaniards, the tensions of an embryonic Spanish America, busily combining races and human groups at varying stages of evolution and communication, set off sudden explosions of violence and crime or they sought a crude relaxation in sorcery. Again and again the inquisitional proceedings tell about professional sorcerers who "invoke the name of God for lewd and shameful acts, who utter devout prayers, make deals with the Devil, tell fortunes with beans, and the like."

In another respect the Inquisition followed a restrictive policy in the colonies, affecting their intellectual culture. The defensive system of the Spanish Counter Reformation had taken elaborate precautions against the spread in the Indies of even the slightest echoes of the great schism agitating Europe. Ever since 1543 the crown had forbidden the exportation to America of "books of fiction and on secular matters or of fanciful character such as the Amadis romances of chivalry." The highest aspiration of the Counter Reformation ideal was to transform the colonies into an immense meeting house for prayers and devotions. The whole of paragraph xiv of the Laws of the Indies deals with the expurgation of books, and another law requires that "no book dealing with the Indies be allowed, permitted, or printed without special licence of the Council of the Indies." When a ship arrived in port, royal officers made a careful inspection to ascertain whether it carried any works of a forbidden nature, as set forth in the Inquisition's list of prohibited writings.*

It is interesting that the two most delightful narratives by seventeenth-century authors born in Spanish America were composed far away from the Indies. One was the *Royal Commentaries of the Incas* (1609) by the Inca Garcilaso de la Vega, a masterpiece of colonial prose, and the other was the *Historical Account of the Kingdom of Chile* (1646) by a Jesuit, Alonso de Ovalle. As the Inca Garcilaso looked back nostalgically from his long years in Spain to the colorful yet sad fairy tale of his childhood in Peru, the impact on his sensitive, poetic nature of the two heritages in his blood striving to blend

---

* Recent studies have demonstrated, with abundant documentary evidence, that books of all kinds save Lutheran Bibles, tracts, and other Protestant literature, plus a few secular works mainly of geographical nature, circulated with remarkable freedom throughout the former Spanish American colonies during most of the three centuries of Spanish rule. A closer scrutiny of the legislation here mentioned indicates that it was intended to keep fictional works out of the reach of the Indians who were learning Spanish and who, in their unfamiliarity with literature and writing, might easily confuse fiction with fact. The enlightened effort of the Spaniards to make the Indians and mixed elements literate on a large scale soon subsided, and the ban against the circulation of fictional writings, never primarily aimed at the American-born Spaniards, quickly became inoperative and a dead letter. During the colonial centuries the great majority of the works banned and expurgated were ecclesiastical and nonsecular, while the book trade between Spain and its possessions prospered greatly with the importation of thousands of volumes annually, including much belletristic literature. See, for example, José Torre Revello, *El libro, la imprenta y el periodismo en América durante la dominación española* (Buenos Aires: 1940); and Irving A. Leonard, *Books of the Brave. Being an Account of Books and Men in the Spanish Conquest and Settlement of the Sixteenth Century New World* (Cambridge: Harvard University Press, 1949). Also, recent works tend to place more emphasis on the police-court functions of the Inquisition, necessary in any society, than on the persecution of heretics, alleged or otherwise. (Translator's note.)

within him infused the pages of his *Royal Commentaries* with a
tender melancholy. Over them was diffused a gentle mist of recol-
lection that invested everything he wrote with a slightly muted,
never strident, charm. And, similarly, the Chilean Ovalle, in his
retreat at Rome, turned his thoughts to the mountain scenes, to
guanaco hunting expeditions, his journeys astride a donkey along
the narrow trails of the Andes, and to the lush greeness of the
Aconcagua valley. From these memories he extracted his delightful
Historical Account which has more interest as poetry than as history.
The enchantment of distance moved them to conjure up the light
and the color of American landscapes from their own minds. Had
they remained in the Indies, not only the emotions of these two
writers might have been weaker, but they might not even have sensed
the wonder and uniqueness of distant places.

Royal decrees and the policies of the Inquisition hushed the colonial voice. Since it was not permitted to write novels or histories
concerning the aboriginal inhabitants, it meandered off into the tortuous byways of baroque prose. The frustrated intellectual hid his
repressions behind a tangled shrubbery of verbalism and of excessive
word play in which meaning evaporated in stylistic involutions.
When the Chilean Francisco Núñez de Pineda Bascuñán (1607–
1680) in his *Happy Captivity* told of his life as a captive among the
Araucanian Indians and, in a lively fashion, described their savage
raids and pastimes, the obligatory tedious moral reflections, quotations from the Gospels and from the lives of the saints, and stories
of miracles aborted a potentially excellent novel. Likewise, that likable seventeenth-century gossiper, Juan Rodríguez Freile, author of
El Carnero (The Mutton), a chronicle of New Granada and particularly its capital Bogotá, carefully balanced his juicy anecdotes of
scandal and roguery with pedantic allusions to the Bible and to
theology—matters in which, be it said, the writer seems delightfully
untutored. A restrained jocoseness runs through Rodríguez Freile's
narrative despite the prim, conventlike atmosphere in which it was
written as he writes about witches, rascally soldiers, and frivolous
affairs of the heart. This chronicle of Bogotá offers material for many
tales of passion or for dramatic skits even though, bowing to the

prejudices and hypocrisy of the time, it seeks a pious disguise. This was the maximum liberty a writer could take in that age, at least in the remote colonies of Spanish America. This overly strict and repressive tendency probably explains why Spain's realistic genius, whose mature fruit were the tales of roguery, remained in a larval state, for colonial letters did not produce a single novel. But there were incipient ones in the long, versified narratives of the sixteenth century such as Saavedra Guzmán's *Pilgrim of the Indies*; later, in Pineda y Bascuñán's and Rodríguez Freile's efforts; and finally, toward the end of the eighteenth century, in the *Guide of Blind Travelers*, Concolorcorvo's slightly acidic descriptions of local customs.

But in the seventeenth century—the period of repression *par excellence*—wordiness, affectation, and the retreat from reality prevailed far more than any direct testimony of persons or things, or any literature of action properly speaking. Permeating our attitude toward life and our ways was that strange, historical complex called the baroque.

The Baroque of the Indies

VI

BAROQUE COMPLEXITY AND ITS CONTRADICTIONS

No period is so complex or so varied in its inner contradictions as the baroque, particularly the baroque of Spain. Spanish culture had entered an era of intense feeling with a strong predilection for profuse detail—an era characterized by vital energy in high tension; yet it also exhibited a tendency to draw away from the definite and the concrete. In form this Spanish expression displayed a bold modernism, whereas in content it favored an extreme orthodoxy. This propensity to pair opposites, or to superimpose one upon the other acquired, in some mysterious manner, the designation "baroque." In discussing this peculiar style it is not enough to isolate each individual trait, nor to say as Jacob Burkhardt does, for example, that it is "architecture that starts to make contortions," nor that it is a wall covered with queer details that disturb the onlooker and estrange him from the tranquil vision that Greek or Renaissance composition had offered him; nor is it enough to say that it is dynamic and repetitive, contrasting with the static and classic; nor that it is pictorial in contrast to lineal as in Wölfflin's categories; nor again is it accurate to say that in literature all this means obscurity and clever verbal effects as opposed to the simplicity and clarity of classical expression. All these are attempts to interpret an intricate complex. The baroque that seems warm, sensual, and a little frolicsome in the churches of Naples and in Bernini's fountains, and the baroque in

Austria and Central Europe that was courtly and aristocratic *par excellence*—an art of palaces and gardens or one of the floridity with which the Jesuits reared gilded domes to celebrate their political triumphs and influence over princes—these types of baroque expression took root in Spanish soil as a national style. So far as Spain was denying more modern concepts or was construing them differently, its artistic expression was anti-Renaissance and anti-European. Or perhaps it could be said that Spain was skipping the Renaissance entirely. Under baroque influence Spain was evolving some attitudes or ideas that were not fully developed in the Middle Ages, that is, some of the attributes of chivalry, a somber solace in the thought of death, or again an exuberant rusticity like that of the archpriest of Hita three centuries before. A slightly degenerate chivalry together with undisguised crudity, or an almost refined coarseness visible at times in Francisco de Quevedo's writings; a lofty mien and manner together with cruel mockery; great deference and an easy-going irreverence—all these opposites flourished in counterpoint in this age that knew neither moderation nor a middle ground. The baroque underwent further changes in Spanish America because of a more primitive environment and the hybrid influences that were inevitable in the collision of races and the violence of transplantation.

What is still needed, among other things, for an understanding of these peculiarities is a complete history of Hispanic culture. Through shortsightedness or other limitations Spaniards and Spanish Americans alike have preferred to confine cultural studies to their own localities. Occasionally the Spanish critic Menéndez y Pelayo cast a paternal, admonitory glance at Spanish American culture. For example, he wrote on the history of our poetry with great acumen in some chapters and hurriedly in others. But he could never quite shake off an air of being a teacher who wishes not merely to instruct his overseas pupils but to correct their mistakes. In the interesting historical case of Sister Juana Inés de la Cruz, Menéndez y Pelayo gives much more attention to her exact use of language than to herself as a peculiar phenomenon. And it would seem that he read precipitately. Other Spanish studies tend to emphasize regional limitations, and they hardly dwell on the problems of Spanish culture in

America when they discuss such important if intermittent visitors to Madrid as Ruiz de Alarcón, the Mexican dramatist, or Rubén Darío, the great modernist poet from Nicaragua. But neither have we Spanish Americans dug very deeply into these questions of our origin owing to our prejudices. Whether the latter are liberal or conservative they have been equally negative, either because of a bias against Spain growing out of an adolescent nationalism, or because of a colonial-minded idealization of the mother country. The pre-Independence period, especially the baroque era, offers the historian none of the abundant external details of the Conquest, and its reality, lying deep within, calls for the keenest psychological penetration. Consequently, this part of our past is the least known and the most misunderstood of our whole historical and cultural evolution. The baroque, however, was one of the elements that remained rooted in our culture for a very long time. Indeed, in spite of nearly two centuries of rationalism and modern criticism, we Spanish Americans have not yet emerged fully from its labyrinth. It still heavily influences our esthetic sensibility and the many complex aspects of our collective psychology.

THE BAROQUE IN HISTORICAL PERSPECTIVE

From one point of view the baroque era is a period of extraordinary vitality. Recall, for a moment, the infernal din and clamor of Quevedo's *Visions*, or the wealth of sensory detail, even the coarsest and most intimate, of which Spanish picaresque literature was replete. Owing to its zestful vitality and exuberance the baroque was a time of hyperbole and superlatives. "My song is a flood," wrote Quevedo in a famous verse of his famous *Epistle*, meaning that it was not enough to sing within the normal range of the human voice because one longed to be a supervoice, a torrent. This psychological state of mind inevitably led to an overstressing of individual style. Ordinary language was inadequate because the idea and its utterance demanded an exceptional or highly individualized expression. Quevedo is, perhaps, the best example of this world of feeling, sensation, and the yearning for still more that obsessed the age. The academic distinction between *conceptismo*, or conceptism, and *culteranismo*, or a high-flown, fustian style, is of no special importance in stating the general problem. Quevedo and Luis de Góngora, who mutually disliked and denied each other, both labored for the same fundamental purpose. This was true even though Quevedo's prose was like a dark etching touched by the blackest and gloomiest tints of the Castilian soul, while Góngora's poetry was musical, pictorial, and brightened by the clear and luminous colors of the Andalusian, Moorish, or Mediterranean landscape. Although one projected his inner world and his conception of ugliness and evil, and the other made use of the most external and mythological elements in his art, they both met on the plane of intense *pathos*. In Góngora's verse as in Quevedo's pages literature tries to be something more than just literature; indeed, in its desire to achieve full feeling, it seems to invade the other arts. Some of Góngora's famous hyperbatons can have no other meaning. *El fresco de los céfiros ruido* (the cool sound of zephyrs) seems a group of words whispering like an evening breeze in the woods, or the phrase of a cantata, just as another hyperbaton *El denso de los árboles celaje* (the thick cloud effect of the trees) is neither more nor less than a brush stroke; in the perfect fusion of the chiaroscuro it is a fragment of a baroque painting. It seems impossible to create a more varied aggregate of sensory impressions— in which not only sight and hearing participate but also the senses of smell, touch, and taste—than the following fragment by Góngora where one might say that, along with delight, one almost feels a slight revulsion from the cloying sweetness of the last verse:

> Sudando néctar, lambicando olores
>
> .   .   .   .   .
>
> cuyos enjambres, o el abril los abra
> o los desate el Mayo, ámbar destilan
> y en ruecas de oro rayos del sol hilan.
>
> Perspiring nectar, distilling odors
>
> .   .   .   .   .   .

Whose swarms, either April opens
or May releases, exude amber
and spin golden sunbeams on distaffs.

To make honey of the sun, spin it into threads like a honeycomb, and make us experience it not only visually but as a sense of taste— this, indeed, is a truly extraordinary baroque metamorphosis. When material reality is impoverished and, as Dámaso Alonso well noted, when it becomes impossible to extract any further sensations from it, then change takes place: it is treated as unreal or as mythical. How does one praise an heir apparent to the throne whose personality is not yet fully matured, without falling into mere politeness or a fawning triteness? Góngora addresses the prince who will become Philip III: "O propitious dawn of the gleaming evening star!" The vagueness of this eulogy is veiled in the oddity of the expression. In the metaphorical world of Góngora's poetry the wind that drives against the leaves is like Jupiter when he comes down to Leda. On the roses that await him the wind descends with "purple wings if lustful breath." To state, however, that, from the esthetic point of view, the baroque was a moment of vital frenzy, of intense yearning, does not explain the whole historical problem. The Renaissance also was powerfully alive. Furthermore, it was free of that feeling of discouragement, dismay, and disillusion that was so typical of seventeenth-century culture. Renaissance vitality, unlike the baroque, always sought a rule or archtype. The "excessive drive," Renaissance pride, and consciousness of power, operated under a regulating intelligence. Every thing had a rule, a special type; for architecture it was Vitrubius and Vignola, for civil life Alberti and Palmieri, and for aristocratic etiquette Baltasar de Castiglione. In Renaissance culture a universalist concept prevailed that acquired the Latin of the Humanists as an international medium. The triumphs of the mind and spirit were won in approximating an ideal model of deportment and beauty such as Platonic philosophy offered, for example, and not in the chimerical solitude that the baroque exalted. Figuratively speaking, the Renaissance was a dialogue, a being together, whereas

the Spanish baroque was mostly a soliloquy—the soliloquy of Segismund in Calderón's *Life is a Dream*. Really, what else is seventeenth-
century Spanish literature but a series of soliloquies that contradict
each other or cancel each other out? The crepuscular symbol of the
age is Segismund in his prison cell with his superimposed images of
reality and illusion that he is unable to disentangle. Segismund seems
to adumbrate the weak, neurotic, fear-haunted Charles II, last of the
Habsburg dynasty, with whom would end the little that remained
of the grandeur that was Spain.

Unlike the Renaissance, the baroque life force wound up by denying life, by forever drawing a line between what was eternal and what
was temporal. It is a significant fact in the history of Spanish American thought that a Guaraní version of Father Nieremberg's *Crucible
of Disillusionment* was read to the Indians in the Paraguayan missions and that this work was one of the first that the Jesuits printed
and illustrated with engravings comprehensible to the simple minds
of the natives.

Another matter marks off the essential difference between the
baroque and the Renaissance. It is the spiritual and intellectual
repression, notably in Italy and Spain, brought about by the Counter
Reformation, whose direct influence on Marinism and the involuted
expression of the Italian seventeenth century Francesco de Sanctis
traced so admirably in the nineteenth. This critic pointed out that,
as soon as the Inquisition was established in Italy, the element of
content dropped out of the disappearing humanism of the Renaissance and extremely mannered formulae took its place. Since new
truths could no longer be stated and the development of science had
come to a standstill, literature became a "verbalized spectacle, a
wholly empty, idle pursuit." Form became cryptic and was worked
over in a highly convoluted manner for two reasons: either because
it had nothing to say or was unwilling to say it, or because it was
necessary to avoid all risk by concealment in a tangled skein of
words. Literature, divorced from any useful or rational content,
seemed to become a language art detached from meaning. Everything was sacrificed to music and bizarre effects. Now it was the time
of *concetti preziozi*, of clever verbal gymnastics. Allegory again

stepped between art and reality, not in the dual sense of two separate worlds—the ideal and the real, as in the Middle Ages—but rather to illumine reality with a new, artificial, or, as we would now say, expressionistic light. Broken is the Renaissance harmony between sensibility and reason.

In the new art of allegory Spanish literature revived the emblem. Gracián clearly defined the surrealist value of emblematic symbols: "These literary conceits are very clever sophisms to set forth the sentiments of the soul with the wildest exaggeration." Wildest exaggeration? Doesn't that really define the vital principle of the baroque? Symbols and metaphors became so indispensable that Juan de Horozco y Covarrubias published his New Art of Propagating Ideas and Images to meet the great demand. The painstaking art of the engraver coöperated with the author in the technique represented by the emblem, and the same tendency appeared in public celebrations, a few of which became important in our cultural history, notably the one held in Lima in 1627. This event, about which the poet Rodrigo de Carvajal penned a detailed chronicle in verse, honored the birth of the royal prince Baltasar Carlos. A mythological carnival procession —the phrase is Ventura García Calderón's—paraded through Lima's streets. Among its features were crocodiles drawn by mules draped with pelts of mythical unicorns, whales, astrologers, Polyphemus with an enormous eye, Ganymedes and Aeneas, Jason in pursuit of the Fleece, Saturn carrying an hour glass, and Mars. Apollo's chariot also appeared bearing an effigy of the poet, Luis de Góngora. This last is an item of extraordinary interest because it indicated that, already in 1627, the fame of the great Cordoban bard had spread throughout the Spanish empire. The fact that, only a few months after his death, the people in the colonies represented him in a float together with Homer and Vergil is clear evidence that Góngora, like the esthetics that he personified, penetrated into the distant fastness of Peru at a very early date.

If symbolism, allegory, and euphuistic language were masks of baroque repression, the irrepressible vitality of the time exploded, by way of compensation, in bursts of crudity, mockery, and cruelty. Some of the heartless gibes that the talented and unlucky Mexican dramatist Ruiz de Alarcón endured, for example, strike us as strange and incredible. Never did social behavior in the literary world fall so low. Typical of the times was the mordant satire in which Quevedo was so gifted. It was present in many of Góngora's random sonnets, in the gossip, slander, and innumerable intrigues that filter through colonial documents, and in the endless petty quarrels within the convents and between the religious orders. Sister Juana Inés de la Cruz could write mocking sonnets or verses in a prearranged rhyming order in which she was not squeamish about using malodorous words or ending lines with references to the digestive process such as "to satiate," "belch," "foul breath," and the like.

Scholastic philosophy, renovated by Suárez and the theologians of the universities of Salamanca and Alcalá de Henares, became the aggressive philosophy of the Counter Reformation and a bulwark against the increasing inroads of European empiricism, criticism, and natural science. Scholasticism, much more than a mere philosophical system, was a way of life, an ethical style, a kind of needle-point canvas on which everything that the man of the age wished to express must be embroidered. This resurrected medieval form now contained the whole of the baroque will. It admirably fitted the ascetic disillusionment of the age and it sustained the spiritual unity of the Spanish world despite political decadence. It was a philosophy *sub specie aeternitatis*, outside of time, compared to the confident realism and the sense of being a part of history then so far advanced in European thought. Why be concerned about mundane things when they are all so transitory, when life is hardly a stage but, rather, a noisy, bustling, half-blind market place, to use Calderón's often quoted simile? In this ephemeral, earthly sphere poor, wretched mankind is merely a plaything of two powerful and, apparently, antagonistic forces that eventually come together: pain and pleasure. Seemingly distinct one from the other they are, perchance, no more than the two faces of a Janus-like force:

> Sorrow stumbles upon me
> when I meet pleasure.

And why not, if man by nature
is the target of both?

And so, amidst the complicated apparatus of scholastic logic and
the perfected art of the syllogism that contemporaries admired in
Calderón's drama, these stage properties created their effects and
projected over the theater a nocturnal glow, a magic phosphorescence.
It had none of mankind's passionate attachment to the earth and
disenthrallment from heaven that Shakespeare exhibited. Man partly
disappears into the whole and the abstract. "Entities that bring together an aggregate of general traits disregard irregularities, peculiarities, and anomalies so as to rise to the common convergence point
of human impulses and conceptions," is the shrewd comment of
Lucian Paul Thomas, a modern interpreter of Calderón. Regarding
the latter's plays, Mendéndez y Pelayo declared: "He exalts the
triumphs of religion over human knowledge and doubt, reason over
the flesh, and free will over unrestrained passion." In the scholastic
and baroque drama of Calderón man's greatest achievement is not
his history but his theology. Theology negates history because
theology presupposes a changeless eternity. From the ethical point of
view man must deny the world in order to approach God. In the
desire to change things, is there not something of childish pride and,
perhaps, a bit of devilish perversity? Is innovation possible, after all,
in an eternal order of theology? Alejandro Korn has acutely observed
that no words in seventeenth-century Spanish thought were so disdained as "novelty" and "innovation." And perhaps the lush intricacy
of form, which moved from literature into scholarship, juridical
discourses, and theological disquisitions, was a natural and understandable substitute for the most dangerous of all "novelties":—ideas.
Seventeenth-century Spain would assert its antimodern consciousness by throwing up a formidable system of spiritual and intellectual
defenses.

The general character of the culture imposed by the mother country acquired added complexity in the Spanish American environment. Since intellectual activity in the colonies was the privilege

of a tiny educated minority devoid of any understanding of the Indian and *mestizo* masses, it had a wholly cryptic character. This small group spent its leisure in playing both an aristocratic and erudite game in which the bizarre and strange became a part of the pastime. As the great epic of the Conquest was a thing of the past and life in the viceregal capitals had settled into a routine, this luxury and refinement lay superimposed upon the semibarbaric immensity of the land. Protestant pirate raids on the unprotected coasts hardly ruffled the monotony of colonial existence which, resting on the dual platform of a paternalistic state and a watchful Church, enjoyed the abundance of resources and the cheap labor of aboriginal masses. The Indians had lost their history, as yet the mixed elements had made none, and the little of historical significance that happened was limited to a tiny circle of half-alien whites in whom a national consciousness had not yet dawned. The pomp and circumstance of the Church, state, and scholastic learning obscured the vision of the world around it from the still unshaped Creole mind. In contrast to the Anglo-Saxon settlements to the north, the Spanish colonies in the south had an urban character. Architecture was the liveliest art in the colonial cities of Mexico, Peru, and Guatemala, because the Spaniards felt a need to match a new splendor against the former glories of the Indians so as to displace their pagan gods; and also because, as historians of South American art have pointed out, the natives played an important role in these creative endeavors—they have left the mark of their own artistic expression on the Spanish Catholic baroque. It is this native influence which has fixed a pale and mysterious beauty upon the two viceregal capitals and also upon Puebla, Oaxaca, and the remote Andean cities of Puno, Juliaca, Huancavelica, Ibarra, Cuenca, and Popayán in Peru, Ecuador, and New Granada. Architecture, which achieved its fullest development in Mexico, painting which at Cuzco could depict the Virgin Mary with fresh and delightful religious feeling wearing a broad-brimmed hat and the puffed skirts of a *chola*, or half-caste woman, and the lyric, multicolored sculptures of Ecuador, were the highest collective expressions of the time. And grouped around these major arts, subordinate but supplementing them, were basketry, ceramics, embroidery, and silver work. The old, applied arts of the natives were now beginning to speak a Catholic language. Precious ecclesiastical robes were made by the very ancient techniques of Mexican feather-work, and rainbow-colored processions in miniature were carved on Peruvian gourds. But, in comparison to this happy marriage of the plastic arts, literature had taken on a far more esoteric and alien character.

THE LITERARY BAROQUE IN THE INDIES

The new style of writing was first noted in the Spanish American colonies in the early years of the seventeenth century. An artistic personality such as Bernardo de Balbuena, the chief poet of the period, offers a fairly precise boundary between a literature largely of action inspired by the many deeds performed in the century of the Conquest, and a literature of contemplation. Content yields to form. The latter kind is typical of a society that has become urban and sedentary, prizing color, music, and cleverness. The amiable ab-bot of Jamaica, Bishop of Puerto Rico, and verbose author of the *Grandeur of Mexico City* and of the *Bernardo* suggests a tropical Ariosto, fond of carrying a colorist, descriptive art so far that the epic fades into lyric vagueness—a tendency initiated by the author of *Orlando Furioso*. The epic still retained its preëminence in litera-ture, however, as a hangover of the Aristotelian rhetoric that the Renaissance had exalted, but it had already lost its former verve. The lyric spirit now pervaded epic poems. Their decadence is evi-dent in Spanish American literature as soon as one turns from the dramatic passages of Ercilla's *Araucana* to the more idyllic than mili-tant world of Pedro de Oña's *Arauco Tamed*. While the *Araucana* is the forthright statement of a soldier well acquainted with rhetoric, de Oña's poem is a less spontaneous work in which the recital of war-like deeds frequently slides off into sheer lyricism. When we read Balbuena, the contrast with Ercilla is sharp: No longer does great panoramic art with a central theme and narrative unity prevail; rather there is a marked preference for picturesque detail. Delight and intoxication with color destroy the unity of line and construc-

tion in the work of the author of the *Grandeur of Mexico City*.
Verbal ornamentation, seeking to free itself from content, is conspicuous like a highly ornate frame. The exploits of Bernardo del
Carpio, or the lively scenes in Mexican streets, squares, and markets
are merely a pleasant excuse for painting pictures. Words have scents
like Oriental spices and sparkle like a mythical treasure. The passage
"pearl, silver, gold, coral, incense, and cinnamon," appears repeatedly
in Balbuena's diction. His eye, as Quintana has noted, is so all-
embracing that it is not selective but transmits, with equal delight,
everything that it views—natural phenomena, fruits, buildings,
theological systems, animals, utensils, or heraldry. Already he is one
of the creators of the fanciful geography that was so typical of the
Spanish baroque. Long before the Romantics, the seventeenth-
century Spaniards embarked upon this picturesque flight through
terrestrial space. If Balbuena sings about Mexico he does so, aside
from its own colorfulness, because the first breath of the Far East
is felt there—because the Manila galleon touches its west coast at
Acapulco. As the seventeenth century dawns Mexico lies on the exact
meridian where the most exotic regions overlap and it is also the
point from which they radiate:

> Peru's silver, Chile's gold
> here converge; fine clove
> from Terrenate, and Tidor's cinnamon,
> fabrics from Cambray, Quinsay's ransome,
> Sicily's coral, Syria's spikenard,
> incense from Arabia, and garnets from Ormuz.

In this moment of esthetic history Horace and Vergil are no longer
the favorites of classic antiquity that they were a few years before
but, rather, the perfumed Ovid. Was not Ovid the most baroque of
the Roman poets when, in his own fashion, he substituted his
amatory art and his artificial elegance for the historical and religious
purpose of Vergil? The likable Diego Mexía de Fernangil, one of the
most appealing figures in Spanish American literature of the time,
made hazardous trips about the continental mainland, translating
Ovid as he went. A delightful novel could be written about his ad-

ventures: His arduous travels included shipwrecks, disastrous business
ventures, and journeys, to quote his own words, over "rough trails,
quagmires, and desert sands through half-starved villages, malarial
fevers, and widespread pestilence." After the loss of his ship in a
harbor of Sonsonate he solaced himself, during the long overland
trip to Mexico City, by reading and translating the *Heroidas*. And
the anonymous woman poet of Peru, author in 1608 of a *Discourse
in Praise of Poetry*, whom Mexía had taught to love Ovid, sent him
her compliments in behalf of "the nymphs of the South," calling
herself his female Phoebus. Much in evidence, too, in the work of
another anonymous woman poet who, under the pen name Amarilis,
had written her well-known epistle in 1621 to the Spanish dramatist
Lope de Vega, are the same fanciful geography and colorful exoticism
so common in Balbuena. From afar she would proffer Lope, her
"Belardo," this lavish and scented tribute:

> Balsam and perfumes from the two Arabias,
> diamonds from Cambaya, gold from Tibar,
> ivory from Sofala, and Persia's treasure.
>
> .   .   .   .
>
> Exquisite coral from the Red Sea,
> spinel rubies from Ceylon,
> precious aloe from Sarnaos and Campanes,
> rubies from Pegubambe, and civet from Nubia,
> amethysts from Rarsinga,
> and fortunate events from Acidalia.

Thus, tidings from the strange and imaginary lands of Sofala,
Rarsinga, and Pegubamba reached Lope de Vega in the verses of an
anonymous poet just as long years before similar ones had come to
the ears of Don Quixote.

Hence, even in colonial Spanish America, the dawning of the
baroque reflected that same eager interest in the exotic and in a
colorful geography that had moved Góngora to write rondelets in
Portuguese, and to parody the speech of African slaves beginning to
talk Spanish, in which, three centuries ahead of time, he wrote
verses that sound today like the lyrics of a rumba. Are not these

lines of Góngora, for example, written in 1609, like a premature rumba?

> Pongamos fustana
> e bailemo alegra;
> que aunque samo negra,
> sa hermosa tu.
> Zambambú, morenica del Congo,
> zambambú.
> Vamo a la sagraria, prima,
> veremo la procesión.

ARISTOCRATIC AND ESOTERIC LITERATURE

As the eagerness for color, cleverness, and the exotic lessened concern for content and focused attention on form, literature, thus stripped of popular expression and social meaning, soon degenerated into an aristocratic and academic pastime. In Spanish America universities and convents became experimental laboratories of esthetic debasement. With its labyrinthian syntax and word play, and its lush effusion of verbal contrivances the baroque fashion overwhelmed the pulpits, university chairs of law and theology, and scholastic dissertations with a dense growth of verbiage. It bestowed incomprehensible titles even on treatises dealing with law, legislation, and mathematics. *The Union of Two Knives* is the name of a work in which Bishop Gaspar de Villaroel made a study of the attributes of Church and State in New World society. The learned Mexican, Carlos de Sigüenza y Góngora, thought up the most extravagant titles for his pamphlets and treatises such as *Astronomical and Philosophical Libra, Mathematical Bellerophon Against Astrological Chimera,* and the like, in his polemic with the Jesuit Father Kino over the nature of comets and against the age-old superstitions of astrology.

The seventeenth-century colonial mind, to which were forbidden the new critical and experimental methods coming into vogue in Europe, was unable to determine the exact boundaries between the different sciences. Its concept of knowledge was a piling up of data rather than a synthesis. The rigidly deductive method of scholasticism did not equip colonial intellectuals with the systematic mind that could understand the special case or could determine the concrete meaning concealed behind a screen of clichés and figures of speech. Striking instances of this condition are the two giants of learning that this baroque culture produced, the Mexican Sigüenza y Góngora and the Peruvian Pedro Peralta y Barnuevo. From reading widely, glimmers of the new scientific learning of Europe had reached them, but their acquaintance with it was not substantial enough to shatter the mold of the older way of thinking. Sigüenza y Góngora tried on occasion to reconcile Biblical lore, Greek mythology, and the Mexican gods. In one of his treatises he propounds the curious thesis that Poseidon must have been the son of Misraim, grandson of Cam, and great-grandson of Noah, and the progenitor of the Indians of the New World. With exemplary care he collected and described many artefacts of Mexican archaeology, but he conjectured that the mythical Quetzalcoatl had been confused with the Apostle Saint Thomas. And with the same criteria Peralta Barnuevo talked about the journeys of Bacchus in Spain and tried to rationalize all the myths in his voluminous and indigestible *History of Spain Vindicated*. Even more absurd were the efforts of a strange clergyman in Guatemala, Friar Diego Saenz de Ovecuri, who brought into play all the standard verbalistic tricks and devices in his *Thomasiada*: ballads that rhymed by omitting vowels, conundrums, and hieroglyphics—contrivances that seem like forerunners of modern calligrams, or poems contained within a geometric pattern. His mania reached a peak when, aiming to be both ingenious and pedagogical, he earnestly wished to assemble every subject in logic, philosophy, metaphysics, speculative, and moral theology in a "sphere of verse."

What might be called the esthetic will of the time was significantly set forth in the *Apologetics in Defense of Góngora*, ably written by an educated *mestizo*, Juan de Espinosa Medrano, the "Pock-marked," and possibly the most interesting work of literary criticism produced in the whole colonial period. Espinosa Medrano writes at times with a style worthy of Gracián when he says, for example, that "the bulk of a book merely indicates that there is a lot of paper in it," and when he puns that "volumes grow to bear fruit, not to put out leaves, which is their only remaining relation to trees." In his short treatise praising Luis de Góngora he develops two basic ideas: why art should be strange and uncommon, that is, different from the ordinary run of things, and why *belles lettres* should differ from theology, or why the beauty of the sacred differs from the beauty of the profane. In explaining and justifying Góngora's use of the hyperbaton he remarks, for example, that it is common to all poetry since, even etymologically, the word "verse" is derived from "reversing terms, inverting style, and intermingling (*entreverar*) words." He notes that, by means of the hyperbaton, the Cordoban bard achieves effects of intensity, color, and melody that are impossible in a strictly logical word order. The great merit of Góngora—whom he calls the "big giant," "the divine Daedalus"—rests on the fact that "he recast the sentence, stimulated eloquence, and seasoned witty sallies." To defend Góngora in the matter of the difference between the beauty of the sacred and the beauty of the profane, Espinosa Medrano also wrote: "On seeing the richness of the Sacraments, the Apostle declared that the sacred scriptures were hidden in earthen pots made of unadorned words; we keep the precious treasure inside fragile vessels of clay when, in contrast, all the majesty of mundane writings consists in having the pots inside the soul and the tinsel outside." This means that the sacred is a mystery and therefore requires no embellishment. Art, a creation of the human mind, starts from "what is little more than nothing at all, from an epigram, from a flash of wit" and becomes a mystery through its form.

SATIRE, MOCKERY, AND NON-CONFORMITY IN THE BAROQUE

But such esoteric matters are only one aspect of colonial culture. The historian who limits his attention merely to this decorative tendency, to the exceedingly formal and aristocratic tone of most literary works of the seventeenth century, will fail to comprehend the inner contradiction, the repressed passion, the real spiritual drama of the period, which is thus concealed. Contrasting with the strict conventions of formal literature mechanically produced by the universities and convents and manufactured for religious occasions and ceremonial events, the colonies occasionally permit a glimpse of a more hidden or tragic facet of literary life. Notable instances are Juan del Valle Caviedes in Peru and, even more conspicuously, Sister Juana Inés de la Cruz. An acid view of life, a reality quite unlike that reflected in the conventional art, crops out in the grim humor of Caviedes and in the stately, metaphysical drama of Sister Juana. Utterly different in quality and in their modes of expression these two figures are, for my taste, the most interesting and, perhaps, the most frustrated in colonial literature of the late seventeenth century.

Juan de Caviedes represents the reaction of the popular to the mannered and overly artificial. His *Tooth of Parnassus,* whose poems in ten-line stanzas are like etchings depicting everyday life in seventeenth-century Lima, is typical of one who is reacting to a situation. He is resentful because he does not enjoy official acceptance, because he is a nobody in the capital. Having no university degree, he can neither view the passing parade from the vantage point of the ornate auditorium of an institution of learning, nor from that of an aristocratic drawing room. Instead he, a peaked little shopkeeper, looks out on the world from his dull and dingy shop near the river. He is a minor Quevedo, far less tutored and also less misled by bookish learning. The lively, uninhibited strain of picaresque literature seems to have reached Spanish America in his verses. Like his contemporary, Molière, he mocks his own physical sufferings, his disillusionment with quack doctors, and his feelings of frustration. He is baroque much less in the intricacy of his writing—as a talented man of the street he escaped the professorial pedantry of his time —than in the vehemence and violence of his jeers, the crudity of his coarseness, and in a sadistic wallowing in the unpleasant. An obsession with death in a Spanish and medieval manner, a sardonic satisfaction in his physical disintegration, and gloomy disillusionment with life are the subject matters of his mocking verses. When Ricardo Palma rediscovered the writings of Caviedes last century, all that Palma saw in them was the irony and wit of a clever Spanish American; he regarded Caviedes as a representative of the wit common in Lima at the time, a jocose individual who tossed off comic verses. But, if we read him more carefully, the corrosive nature of his bitter humor is more evident. The idea, so thoroughly baroque, that the world is a stage, a bazaar of humbugs cloaked in costumes and of false personalities, runs through his long gallery of caricatures. There are doctors on horseback with their foul-smelling potions and surgeon's lancet in hand bent on blood-letting, flatterers, hypocrites, pious frauds, prostitutes, "stuffed shirts," and learned fakes. In all Spanish American literature there is no poem so cruel, so absolutely disillusioned, whose epigrammatic grace in its eight-syllable lines so accentuates the feeling of scoffing derision as Caviedes's *To Lovely Arnada* in which, with morbid detail [and much word play baffling to a translator] he minutely describes the death of a prostitute in a Lima hospital.

> Arnada was purging her sin in the hospital,
> for the sins of life must be purged in death.
>
> . . . .
>
> She's in the Charity Hospital
> because of her generous charity,
> for she never denied her alms
> to any love that came begging.

THE STRANGE CASE OF
SISTER JUANA INÉS DE LA CRUZ

Sister Juana Inés de la Cruz's work, more than any other, seems to bring into peculiar focus the values and enigmas of the baroque century. She was a precocious Mexican maiden who, at the age of sixteen, astonished the learned men of the viceroyalty by her erudition. When examined in the most varied and recondite matters by a solemn committee in the approved baroque manner, she "disposed of the questions as a royal galleon would beat off attacking sloops," which was the way a contemporary described the incident. Yet she paid her tribute to everyone of the labyrinthian complexities of style and fashion current in her day. She composed random verses for special occasions, morality plays, Christmas carols, tried out new meters, wrote versified medleys, and manufactured hieroglyphic poems. She celebrated the arrival of a viceroy with the baroque *Allegorical Neptune, Ocean of Colors and Political Image* but, in spite of the degenerate esthetic atmosphere which she breathed, she managed to strike one of the most personal and fascinating lyric notes in all Spanish American poetry. Scholastic philosophy, music, mathematics, and the subtle psychological analysis of current Jesuit theology, all found a place in the baroque content of her verse. But her personal life was a heart-rending drama of repression and disillusionment that, unlike Caviedes's, had no outlet or escape valve in bitter mockery and grim realism. Rather, she seemed to armor herself with a proud shield of logic and metaphysics. Few works of Spanish American poetry have the intellectual content that hers have. By arguments arranged like syllogisms she tries to convey to us the anguish of her heart. In the drama of life she lifts her proud summons, like the Cassandra of one of her poems, for a clear perception and understanding against the stupor that enthralls the senses:

> It sought Cassandra's fierceness
> and cruelly tied the hands of reason,
> the sovereign princess of the soul.
> Her beauty a captive of bold-minded soldiers,
> she mourned the unbelieved disasters
> that she foresaw,
> for however loud her cries,
> the senses did not heed her.

This pride and renunciation were not achieved without destroying her own inner vitality, and in the few of her truly lyric lines, which are in contrast to her verses of logical reasoning, we may measure the pain of her frustration:

> Enough of sufferings now, my dear, enough;
> let neither the tyranny of jealousy torment thee,
> nor vile fear tarnish thy virtue with foolish shadows
> and unsubstantial signs,

for thou hast seen and held my heart between thy hands
dissolved in the fluids of the body.

The Góngora-like solitude in its mythological setting becomes
stripped and bare in Sister Juana, for she has to some extent re-
nounced the cheerful background of nature for the total solitude of
an abstract idea or, as Abreu Gómez puts it, for the "solitude of soli-
tudes." Having rejected action, she seeks to be a witness of the "civil
war of the soul," that "scene of the second Troy." The scholastic
method enables her to clarify the labyrinths of the soul much as
psychological introspection in the Jesuit manner teaches her to map
out and describe them. Basically her poetry is to set up dilemmas,
to make pronouncements on questions like these: Which is better,
to love by choice or by stern necessity? Or again, How may beauty
which is importuned reject the proffered love and retain the esteem
and good will of the suitor in spite of the rebuff? She uses Jesuitic
methods set forth in the *Exercises* of Saint Ignatius Loyola to determine the indispensable plastic elements in her poetry. Imagination
links situations together in a strictly logical order and animates the
stage upon which the struggle of the soul's powers is enacted. Hence
her psychological subtlety and even her casuistry oddly coincide with
the Spanish theology of the time. When she is not interpreting this
drama and when she only wishes to relax or play, she does not turn
to the gaiety of nature, nor even to the genuine verbal delight of
"words like brush strokes" after the manner of Góngora; rather, she
immerses herself in symbols and abstractions. In geometry and music
she looks for what she refuses to demand of life. In complexity she
finds calm. She spins spiral convolutions in the world of the abstract,
as she herself explains:

> Harmony is a spiral and not a circle.
> Because it twines above itself
> I named it "snail"
> since it makes this convolution.

The *sub specie aeternitatis* of scholasticism mingles with the ascetic
disillusionment of the age. Beauty's danger, says Sister Juana, is that

it is usually scorned once it is possessed. And she, the much frustrated lover, reminds the satisfied lover:

> Soon thou wilt weep over thy jealousy
> and vainly will thy song be sung,
> for thou dost not heed in thy sad state
> that the end of thy joy
> will be the beginning of thy pain.

Thus the baroque "excess" reaches the limit of disillusion and death. In the world of syllogisms and frozen logic where her life lies buried Sister Juana permits herself now and then, as if to offer an excuse, to listen to "the rhetoric of grief." No other artist suffered nor better expressed the tragic drama of the artificiality and repression of our Spanish American baroque than did this extraordinary Mexican nun.

Baroque Learning,
Issues, and Books

VII

THE SCHOLASTIC PATTERN OF
COLONIAL CULTURE

When Spanish authoritarians imposed scholastic philosophy on university life during the Counter Reformation, they deliberately tried to ignore the new experimental and natural sciences, the *saggi de naturali esperienza*, already beginning to engage the attention of the rest of Europe. Spain's backwardness in science was not the result of unawareness or indolence but, rather, of an adverse inclination, sufficiently suspicious that, when it came to choosing between science and religion, the balance swung to the latter for political and intellectual reasons. The problem of Hispanic culture was then identified with a determination to preserve the ways of an aggressive Catholicism in a Europe torn by dissension. Sixteenth-century Spain had plainly demonstrated that it was in no way inferior to other Western peoples, for its mathematicians and cosmographers, from Fernández de Enciso to Martín Cortés, had made important contributions to the new sciences of navigation and geography, its military engineers had advanced the techniques of warfare (particularly in fortifications and artillery), and its metallurgists had facilitated a rapid and profitable exploitation of mines at the great centers in Mexico and Peru. It should be recalled that the amalgamation of silver with mercury, the most significant metallurgical discovery of the time, grew from the experiments of Álvaro Barba at the Potosí mines who later published his findings in his *Art of Metals* (1640).

The way Spanish thought reacted to the flurry of Renaissance criticism, sensed the problems of the new age, and noted the urgency of a new methodology to replace a purely medieval authoritarianism is apparent in a curious treatise entitled *Naturae Historia prima in magne operis* by Benito Árias Montano. But the Counter Reformation barred the way that might have connected Spain with the natural and experimental sciences rapidly developing in Europe. *Nostram Philosophia debere Christianam esse ac divinae theologiae ministram*, Francisco Suárez had said, and so scientific content was subordinated to the theological ideal. The experimental approach to truth was rejected because, within the scholastic concept, human reason, which was but a pale reflection of divine intelligence, could only know and reproduce absolute forms. The pedagogy of the time chiefly sought a method of disputation rather than a method of observation. What really mattered was to adapt things to the accepted norm, which was regarded as the highest; therefore from this philosophic intellectualism another characteristic of the colonial mentality may be deduced, namely, the denial of progress because the divine order is regarded as immutable. The colonial mind wished to live in a world unaffected by things temporal and accidental and it therefore lacked the historical spirit, that is, a consciousness of change. The particular was subordinated to an ideal principle, to a standard of authority or tradition not experimentally demonstrated.

In opposition to the new learning which, as Galileo had shown, was based on a continuous *provando e riprovando*—that is, acceptance or rejection through experimentation—the scholastic system dominating seventeenth-century Spanish thought rested on the following postulates as explained by Cardinal Ceferino González, a modern apologist of Hispanic scholasticism:

1. Utilize the Aristotelian methods for an orderly and coherent arrangement of all doctrines and opinions established by the Church Fathers. Since patristic literature had sprinkled, so to speak, its theories and interpretations of dogma over the Faith, now a more disciplined method of discussion was sought. In polemics the first step is

to explain the proposition to be established, then to refute opposing opinions and, finally, to reaffirm the thesis desired to prevail.

2. The concept of "revealed knowledge" is superior to all and any experimental analysis. No experiment is valid that is contrary to revelation. God is the primary source of all things, intrinsic and extrinsic. Philosophy must decide and solve fundamental problems in a manner consistent with revealed knowledge. The intellect must do its best to explain, confirm, and demonstrate the revealed truths that are not beyond the reach of human reason. For the truths that are above reason and known only through revelation, philosophy is obliged, as far as possible, to show the connection between them and matters within the range of our experience and reasoning power. In the inevitable conflict of reason and Faith, the latter prevails over the former. *Fides quaerens intellectum* Saint Anselmo had declared.

3. In the dualism of soul and body, the first rules the second. The soul, which is immaterial, does not have its effective cause in man but in God who created it from the void. The intellect has an almost exclusive primacy among the faculties of the soul, since it is a specific quality of man. In offering a graduated scale from nature to divinity Pope Saint Gregory declared that man has his existence in common with stones, his being with plants, and his mind with angels. This scholastic idea made use of the Aristotelian distinction of matter and form. Matter was the actual but purely passive and indefinite principle, whereas form was the active principle which animated and conditioned matter.

The writings of colonial scholars reveal a conflict by submitting what they observed to scholastic scrutiny, a difficulty compounded by the criteria of authority. To no other type of learning is Kant's aphorism quite so applicable which states that, when the boundaries of a science are crossed and another is invaded, the result is denatured rather than increased knowledge. Hesitating between science and Faith and disdaining the methods and instruments of measurement that the Renaissance mind had begun to apply to the study of the physical world, the colonial scholar was caught in a labyrinth. The Mexican Sigüenza y Góngora and the Peruvian Peralta Barnuevo were striking examples of this dilemma. Even though something of what was going on in the European world of science reached them through their wide reading, they had no means for extracting final conclusions.* In Sigüenza y Góngora's famous polemic with the Jesuit Father Kino, recently arrived from Europe, and with other Mexican opponents on the subject of the comet of 1680 which had aroused so much terror throughout the viceroyalty, he well knew that these apparitions were neither a cause nor an indication of calamities to come as the Jesuit was asserting, nor that they were made "by exhalations of dead bodies and human perspiration," but he still did not rise entirely above the superstitious astrology of his time. Even at the close of the colonial period during the last decades of the eighteenth century when modern physics began to enter Spanish American universities, it was not so much the substitution of one system for another as a jumbling of medieval cosmology and ideas borrowed from Newton and Kepler. In a treatise on physics which Father Elías del Carmen prepared in 1784 for his students at the Córdoba Academy in Argentina, several of the topics for study were like the following: whether God is chaos in its vastness or whether He is the spacial form itself of matter, or whether He is in the space outside of the world; also, whether angels and demons through their own properties can move bodies physically; and whether bodies can penetrate each other mutually by divine reason just as the body of Jesus Christ passed through the stones of his sepulchre, and the like.

In its effort to fuse (*reducire ad unum*) such unlike things as science and revelation, the colonial mind tended to find a way out through mysticism. The aged Peralta Barnuevo, who had been a

---

* Sigüenza y Góngora used a telescope "of four lenses which, up to now, is the best that has reached this city," with which he made careful observations of comets and eclipses of the sun, exchanging his observations with scientists in Europe. His *Astronomical and Philosophical Libra* (1690), based on these observations on comets and mathematical calculations, is remarkably modern in some respects, and his familiarity with Cartesianism is clearly evident in numerous citations. Peralta Barnuevo in Lima also possessed a telescope and was competent in applied mathematics. He corresponded with European scientists on astronomical matters, and his observations of eclipses of the moon were published in Paris in the *Histoire de l'Academie Royale des Sciences*, of which institution he was a corresponding member, in 1717 and 1731. (Translator's note.)

cosmographer and mathematician, had superintended the construction of fortifications in Lima, and who, with unquenchable curiosity, had written on all sorts of subjects, set forth his ultimate disillusion with the world in a strange work *Passion and Triumph of Christ*, perhaps the best product of his baroque quill, in which he seems to bewail his disenchantment with all learning and the universal dominion of death. True wisdom, that is, the inscrutable knowledge of God, is not "subject to human comprehension," writes this Peruvian in his song of Ecclesiastes, and Providence is governed "by rules often opposed to the means."

THE "SURPRISE AND WONDERMENT" OF AMERICA. FATHER ACOSTA'S WORK

The strangeness of the New World undoubtedly subjected the mind of the time, steeped in scholastic and patristic philosophy, to questions and problems with which its background of European tradition could hardly cope. The hypotheses of ancient works and Christian tradition concerning the nature of the world were beset by unforeseen ambiguities when applied to new and different surroundings. Did the Indians descend from Adam? Did they not constitute a lesser line of descent, and were they not slaves by nature as Aristotelian thinkers proclaimed? How could the peopling of America be reconciled with the Biblical version? How could such descendants of Adam and Eve have reached such out-of-the-way regions? How was it that the Torrid Zone was habitable despite what Aristotle had said, and why did people not walk upside down at the antipodes? These were among the frequent questions that came up when the attempt was made to incorporate America into ideas and beliefs current in Christian Europe. While the earliest chroniclers, such as Gonzalo Fernández de Oviedo, had been content to list and describe its peculiarities, the philosophic mind of Father José de Acosta, at the end of the sixteenth century, tried to confront the whole problem of America. The *Natural and Moral History of the Indies* by this famous Jesuit, published in Seville in 1590, is first-rate evidence of the evolution of our culture not only for its elegant style, its abundant data, and the

wide range of topics, but also for its discreet hints of a conflict between truth and traditional prejudices. In this excellent work America
is sensed as an exciting array of problems. His solid classical learning,
mastery of contemporary geography and mathematics, keen eye for
historical and social aspects, and the rigorous questioning to which
he subjects everything he observes, together with his extensive travels
from Mexico to Peru, are all useful to him in comparing the reality
of America with the theories about the nature of the world set forth
in ancient works. He is fully aware of his purpose, which is not to
add one more description to the many existing ones but "to deal with
the causes and reasons for the differences." Analysis prevails over
narration. The objects of his book are: A theory of the nature of the
New World and its societies, and a critical examination and verifi-
cation of matters that he may be able to correct or explain better.
Why was Lactantius mistaken about the antipodes, and what were
St. Augustine's reasons for denying their existence? Why did he not
grant the validity of the Platonic myth of the lost continent of
Atlantis? And how is it that Peru cannot be identified with the
legendary Ophir of the Scriptures? What is the true nature of the
equinox, and how is the influence of latitude modified in the Torrid
Zone? These are some of the questions to which Father Acosta offers
an answer. And similarly, by including geographical features of climate, vegetation, prevailing winds, ocean currents, religion, and social
history in his over-all synthesis, his book is one of the most rounded
examples of Spanish scholarship at the outset of the baroque period.
The fact that he falls back upon his quality as a clergyman when
his criticism of traditional cosmology threatens to be destructive and
chooses an orthodox solution rather removed from his own line of
reasoning is, of course, the result of the inevitable pressure upon him
of the beliefs of the time. With an admirable phrase, quoting Saint
Paul, he wards off all danger: "We writers should not pursue the
letter that kills, but the spirit that gives life." His steady assurance
and gentle irony can always adopt a different posture on confronting
matters that he is analyzing. "I confess that I laughed and made a
jest of Aristotle's meteors and his learning when I observed that, at
the very moment and spot where, according to his rules, everything

would ignite and become fire my companions and I felt cold." Repeatedly he advises that he is looking for a law or broad knowledge more than just observation: "However lowly a thing may be, the wise man draws wisdom from it; and from the smallest and most despicable creatures one may learn much of great worth and profit."

When it is recalled that the most fantastic notions about the possible origin of America lasted until far into the eighteenth century and that the New World continued to be identified with the Biblical Ophir and the Atlantis of Plato, this Jesuit takes a very modern position by asserting, perhaps for the first time, that mankind must have come into the American continent through the Arctic region. Diplomatically he reconciles this theory with the tradition of the Flood: "When the flood ceased, pairs of animals came forth from Noah's ark where they had been shut up. Some instinctively went to places where it was possible and easier to live, thus forsaking the Old World and going through the Arctic lands to the New World." In Book III, chapter 1, of his work Father Acosta even dreams of a scientific knowledge of the New World equivalent in the description and classification of its peculiarities to what Aristotle and Pliny had given of the Old World. History, philosophy, and theology are all complementary in this great intellectual scheme. This vision is explicitly stated in phrases reminiscent of the lofty elegance of Friar Luis de Granada in his *Symbol of the Faith*:

> Whosoever takes pleasure in understanding the true facts of nature, which are so many and varied, will know the joy that history gives, and it will be all the better history because its facts come not from men but from the Creator. Whosoever goes on to comprehend the natural causes of effects shall know the practice of good philosophy. Whosoever rises still higher in his thinking and gazes upon the Supreme Maker of all these marvels and comes to enjoy His knowledge and grandeur, he shall have, we do declare, contact with the most excellent Theology.

The limits that theology imposed upon him as a good missionary move him to reject what seemed rash and opposed to God's ends in his investigations. Particularly revealing of this attitude is his discussion in Book III, chapter 10, on the possibility of an interoceanic canal at the isthmus of Panama. In his delightful way the Jesuit said:

> Some people have talked about breaking through this seven-league stretch and joining the two seas together so as to make the journey easier to Peru inasmuch as the eighteen leagues between Nombre de Dios and Panama City are more expensive and troublesome than the 2,300 leagues by water. But personally I consider this an idle pretension even without the obstacle they state, for, in my opinion, no human power will suffice to break through the very formidable and impenetrable mountain barrier with its hills and rugged crags strong enough to withstand the fury of the two oceans between which God has placed it. Even if mankind should be able to do this, it would be, in my judgment, very proper to fear Heaven's punishment for wishing to change the works which the Creator, in his wisdom and providence, has ordained in shaping the universe.

Despite his inability to free himself from the preconceptions of his time and clerical profession Father Acosta's work remains the most exciting catalogue of problems relating to the New World that Spanish scientific thought produced at the turn of the seventeenth century. Until Alexander von Humboldt came in the closing days of the colonial period to gather material for his great description of New World geography, probably no one has looked over the Spanish American landscape and its inhabitants with the comprehensive gaze that Acosta did. How inferior to the latter were other Americanists of the seventeenth century, such as Friar Juan de Torquemada, author of the prolix *Monarchy of the Indies* (1612), and Friar Augustín de Vetancourt who wrote *Mexican Scene* (1690)! They do not reveal that steadfast attitude of scientific doubt, analysis, and continuous questioning with respect to the phenomena of the New World that gave Father Acosta's *History* such remarkable vitality. A placid, circumscribed conformity seems to have replaced the Jesuit's vital concern with problems in both Torquemada and Vetancourt, although they were skillful writers. For them Spanish America was a subject for religious exaltation rather than for a study. They deal with secondary data and are unable to take the critical, close view of social or natural phenomena that gave the *Natural and Moral History* such unequaled charm.

BOOKS OF THE PERIOD AND THEIR CLASSIFICATION

After the cultural historian has waded through the vast mass of books with outlandish titles and diction perpetrated by baroque pedantry in the viceregal capitals (of which books Beristain, Nicolás León, Vicente de Paula Andrade, and José Toribio Medina have compiled lengthy bibliographies), he may attempt to classify them. Before starting, however, it is well to remember that the writer of that time (and here the examples of Sigüenza y Góngora and Peralta Barnuevo again come to mind) was usually versed in many subjects and did not divide knowledge into separate compartments as we do today. In the prolific output of these authors the trivial alternated with the serious and the specialized with the merely rhetorical. The variety of subject matter in León Pinelo, for example, runs the gamut from a juridical or theological treatise to a colorful disquisition "on chocolate." Variety of this kind bestows such a bizarre character upon the authors' personalities that it often defies systematic classification. Moreover, the literate colonial was almost always an official, who wrote because he was commissioned or paid to write an account of an *auto de fé* or about solemn ceremonies attending the celebration in Mexico City or Lima of the birth of some prince. Accordingly, the chief fare of these literary effusions were the trivial events of city life or crassest flattery. In 1730 two of Lima's most talented figures, the then aged Peralta Barnuevo and the poet Pedro José Bermúdez de la Torre, tried to outdo each other in describing the feat of the Prince of Asturias in killing a bull that had attacked him. Two stout volumes of tedious verse in royal octaves heavily seasoned with mythological allusions constituted the *Fond Acclamation Applauding the Heroic Feat of the Prince of Asturias in Killing a Bull in a Forest* by Bermúdez de la Torre, and the hardly less exuberant *Panegyric Song or Poems Celebrating the Wonderful Shot by Which the Prince, Our Lord, Felled a Fierce Bull* by Peralta Barnuevo. This eulogistic literature and descriptions of festivities were typical features of viceregal life until the close of the eighteenth century when rationalism and a new critical spirit began to stir the colonial mind.

If we omit an analysis of this useless aristocratic literature, the more valuable works of baroque erudition might be classified as follows:

Theological works were in Latin, usually with a minimum of original commentary on the writings of the great Spanish theologians including Cano, Suárez, and Vitoria. Peruvian authors were: Juan Pérez de Menacho, who composed an extensive commentary on Saint Thomas Aquinas, a treatise on moral theology, and several works relating to public ecclesiastical law and church organization in the Indies; Leonardo de Peñafiel, whose *Disputationum theologicarum, Tractatus de incarnatione Verbi divini*, in eight large volumes, was published in Lyons; and Diego de Avendaño, who wrote *Thesaurus Indicus* and *Problemata Theologica*. The Mexican friars Juan López de Agurto de la Mata and Bernardo de Bazán, also commentators on the *Summa Theologia*, were considered among the most important writers of theological treatises born in the Indies. These figures were confused with the expounders of ecclesiastical law, among whom the most famous was a native of Quito, Gaspar de Villaroel, bishop of Santiago de Chile, whose *Pacific-Ecclesiastical Government and Union of Two Blades, Pontifical and Royal* (1656), seemingly was the most popular commentary on the relationship of Church and State in the Spanish American colonies. Villaroel, an amiable writer, who composed pious fables such as his *Sacred, Ecclesiastic, and Moral Stories*, belongs, nonetheless, among the great evangelizers, for in his religious disquisitions he mingled engagingly biographical lore concerning saints with personal experiences and anecdotes drawn from his extensive travels in Spain and South America.

The ethical debate on the enslavement of the Indians following the discovery of America found an echo especially in the *Thesaurus Indicus* (1668) of the Peruvian theologian Diego de Avendaño, who focused attention on this problem. He said that the Aristotelian theory of "slaves by nature," which Sepúlveda had applied to the Indians in his polemic with Las Casas, would be the cruelest mockery of the Gospel. And with a fervor equal to Las Casas's he also branded the slave trade and Negro slavery as crimes. He noted that even from the point of view of positive law, sales of slaves should have no validity, because no legal title can justify the violation of a natural and inalienable right. Moreover, the *Thesaurus Indicus* contains a criticism of the divine right of kings as European absolutism was applying it and, before Rousseau and Montesquieu, gives a formulation of the concepts of "popular will" and "social contract" as bases of political association. Avendaño indicates a new conception of civil liberty that in the eighteenth century thought was to develop in the writings of the Encyclopedists and in the social humanism of ecclesiastical writers such as Clavijero, Alegre, and others. Indeed, the *Thesaurus Indicus* takes on a marked importance for the study of both theology and the philosophy of law in the colonial period.

In the learning of the time, a humble handmaiden of dogmatic theology was moral theology, which brought forth a series of far more popular works on sins and transgressions of the Faith. As was to be expected, Europe's baroque religiosity influenced colonial writers; it liked the complex analyses and confessional "guides" of such men as Alfonso Ligorio or Francisco Sánchez who, with a detailed and almost sadistic realism, seemed to revel in probing consciences and in minutely describing sinful acts. Some of the manuals for administering the Sacraments are of interest for a study of psychology and customs, because they were written in native languages and imitating the ways of expression and reasoning of the Indians whom the confessors were instructing. Jesuits in Paraguay wrote several of these confessional works, and they illustrated matters of Faith by plates suited to the mentality of the Indians. Typical is Father Bartolomé García's manual in Mexico, 1760, for the missions on the San Antonio River. It provides the Catholic confessor with a series of curious questionnaires for quizzing the aborigines, and it alludes to sexual practices and rites still observed today among tribes of northern Mexico after more than two centuries of missionary work among them. Books of this nature, still only barely studied, constitute an indispensable source for ethnological and social investigation of that period.

The higher manifestations of baroque piety in its important ascetic and mystical writings deserve more consideration than is possible here. As the eminent Spanish critic Menéndez y Pelayo has noted, the best sacred epic in Spanish literature, *The Cristiad* by the Dominican friar Diego de Hojeda, was written in Lima and published in Seville in 1611. This poem, more frequently mentioned than read, unfolds the long theological sequence from Man's creation to his redemption by Christ, and the modern reader may enjoy the alternating of solemn and lyric passages and of divine and human sentiments which Hojeda often masterfully accomplishes in his lengthy "books" in royal octaves. The Calvary scenes and the Dominican's skillful depiction of the metamorphosis of the gentle Mary into the sorrowing Mother transfixed by grief have the vitality and pathetic realism of the best Spanish paintings of the time. This humanized realism in portraying a devout theme after the manner of Zurbarán or Ribera is particularly well achieved in the fine stanzas of Books III to XII. The Oriental solemnity of the Biblical metaphor contrasts with the dramatic action in which one can sense the suffering, thirst, sweat, blood, and tears of the God who was made man. Two other Peruvian writers took up the great theme of the Passion of the Savior: Fernando Valverde, whose magnificent parables in his *Life of Christ* (1688) offer some of the finest prose of the time, and the learned Peralta Barnuevo, whose *Passion and Triumph of Christ* (1738)—a work of his disillusioned old age—betrays his anguished piety.

Familiarity with the Bible and the Gospels gives a special tone to this baroque literature. In the provincial seclusion of Tunja in New Granada an extraordinary nun, Francisca Josefa del Castillo (1671–1742), wrote her *Spiritual Affections*, one of the works of the period best revealing genuine Biblical influence. She filled sheets of convent paper with the bits of intimate odds and ends only recently deciphered that make up her biography, and with short poems on mystical love. The metaphors of the *Song of Songs* reappear in the prose of this nun who, with careless ease and as if she were writing a long letter to God, tells everything that comes to her avid, pious, and at times startled, mind. Though lacking the wisdom and

intellectual pride of Sister Juana Inés de la Cruz, she is far ahead
of the latter in mystical intuition. With much psychological detail,
which may seem morbid but is profoundly sincere, she offers a contradictory impression of her helpless soul, now torn by fear of sin,
now immersed in the ecstasy of God, or amazed at the solitude He
has placed between her and the world. Though her work is hardly
familiar in editions that have begun to appear in recent years, she
is the foremost woman prose writer of our colonial literature. There
is something in the refinement of her introspection and in the gently
poetic tone inherent in her style, even when she touches on trivial
matters, that brings her close to the great masters of mystical prose
like Friar Juan de los Ángeles. Though comparison is really impossible, Gómez Restrepo in his excellent treatment of this nun in his
Colombian Literature explains how closely she coincides with the in-
superable Saint John of the Cross in her description of the mystical
state, "the dark night of the soul," and the joy and panic fear with
which she approaches the presence of God. The great poet and the
little-known Colombian nun drank from the same spring, the *Song
of Songs*; both found in the Biblical poem the language to symbolize
their intensity and mystical rapture.

These religious writers drew their nourishment from the wealth
of the Bible, each with a particular accent. If the lyric warmth of
Mother del Castillo is reminiscent of the *Song of Songs*, her Peruvian
contemporary, Juan de Peralta (1663–1747), made use of the theme
and the grave rhythms of the *Psalms* in his *Three Stages of Heaven*,
while the Chilean Manuel de Lacunza (1731–1801) drew his tragic
sense of the divine from the *Apocalypse*. Thus the style and temperament of the writers are indicated through an affinity of choices.
Of them all Lacunza was the most original. A Jesuit expelled from
his native Chile in 1767, he wrote under the Semitic pen name,
Juan Josafat Ben-Ezra, and published in Italy when he was quite old,
his exceedingly curious *Coming of the Messiah in Glory and Majesty*,
later placed on the Index of Prohibited Books. This enigmatic work
expressed both the logical and poetic intensity of a visionary who
beholds in his own time the coming of the Antichrist, and the
sublimated bitterness of an expatriate Jesuit. He wishes to be a

prophet who startles his reader by his fearful symbols of a new age. His personal plight and that of his Order seem, in his shockingly disturbed fancy, to be converted into a theological drama and a cosmic tragedy. God will return in apocalyptic fury. If He came before as a man who wished to suffer and die, now He would come in "glory and majesty" as a vanquisher. Was there a touch of the Semitic and the heritage of a prophet in the blood of this mysterious Chilean Jesuit who wrote as if he were swept along by some dark, inner current striving to revive in a godless, unbelieving age the heart-rending cogency of the prophecies?

More familiar in tone and harmonizing better with the purpose of edifying the public through "stories and examples" were the many writings about the lives of saints. These claimed a considerable audience in the colonies when so few novels were read and even the romances of chivalry were forbidden. (See note on p. 82.) Partly through ingenuousness, or the absence of the critical spirit, or perhaps simply to exploit the air of fantasy that still hung over the name "America," many chroniclers intercalated stories of miraculous happenings in their accounts. Friar Pedro Simón (1574–1630), with his Andalusian propensity for tall tales, introduced many fanciful elements into his *Historical Information about the Conquest in Northern South America*. The supernatural element, the *deus ex machina*, was often present in the Chilean chronicles of Fathers Diego Rosales and Miguel de Olivares.

But the chief material of this sort in the literature of the time was supplied by the lives and miraculous deeds of missionaries, those soldiers of the "spiritual conquest," such as Pedro de Claver who became an apostle and protector of Negro slaves in Cartagena, Felipe de Jesús who left Mexico to preach the Gospel in the distant seas of Asia, Francisco Solano who reduced the wild Indians of northern Argentina to ways of peace, or Luis Bolaños and an Antonio Ruiz de Montoya who explored the Guaraní country and set up the first civilized establishments in the Paraguayan forests. Several of these men—Ruiz de Montoya, for example—told about their adventures, thus exemplifying that curious Spanish double role of saint and discoverer. A golden legend hovers over their lives as is evident in such works as the *Chronicle of the Twelve Apostles*, and the *Life and Miracles of the Apostle Father Francisco Solano* by Diego de Córdoba Salinas (1643, 2d ed.), the *Life of Pedro Claver* by Alonso de Andrade (1657), the *Star of Lima*, a biography of Santo Toribio Mogrovejo, archbishop of Lima, by Francisco Echave (1688), and the extraordinary religious and geographical account of Ruiz de Montoya (1639), previously mentioned.

Together with the saints of action—the "spiritual conquistadors" —this literature of hagiography liked to array the gentle, contemplative virgins such as "The Rose of Lima," Mariana de Jesús, heroine of that fair legend of shy intimacy that sprinkled its delicate, lyric perfume over the life of the colonial communities. On the cover of one of the most baroque poems by Luis Antonio de Oviedo Herrera, Conde de la Granja, dedicated to Santa Rosa de Lima on the occasion of her canonization in 1711, she is depicted as receiving garlands of flowers from the hands of tiny, playful angels, and a royal palm from an Indian girl symbolizing the New World. *The True Treasure of the Indies* by Juan de Meléndez (1685), offers a wealth of ingenuous fables, cleverly transcribed, that feature the Rose of Lima and the mulatto, Martín de Porres. This book and Juan de Allonza's *Starry Heaven and a Thousand Twenty-Two Model Acts of Mary* (1691), whose naïve cycle of miracles is placed in the Peruvian highlands, are perhaps the two most entertaining works of this kind of literature. The supernatural and miraculous elements in them are balanced by charming touches of local color. Convent dialogues and tales, told in homely language mingling the divine and extraordinary with intimate and realistic touches in a very Spanish manner, give these two books their charm.

The abundant legal and institutional literature of the time can be offered here only in a very general outline. Alejandro Korn has noted that religion, morality, and law as relics of scholasticism and also the desire to subject the whole human order to a divine archetype permeate colonial institutions. Consequently, among the writers of jurisprudence, the boundaries between law and theology are not always clear. "The distinguishing characteristic of this legislation," writes the Argentine philosopher, "is its eagerness to intrude upon the innermost consciousness and establish not only a rule of law but a moral precept based on unchanging ethical values so that human jurisprudence may reflect divine law as indicated by Saint Thomas Aquinas: *Leges quidem justae a lege aeterna, a qua derivantur*."

The echo of the great Spanish theological debates in the sixteenth century—for example, the debate on wars of conquest and the attempt to enslave the Indians—resounds in the works of legal writers. With the vigor of a theologian a lawyer, Francisco Falcón, argued, in the Lima Church Council of 1582, his belief in the purely transitory nature of the semifeudal *encomiendas*. He denied the right of the Spaniards to wage war on the Indians, and he set forth the odd thesis that what was produced within Peru should be consumed there without the imposition of tributes on the natives. According to his legal theory, which was strongly colored by religious radicalism, the propagation of the Gospel was the real reason for the presence of the Spaniards in this far-off world of the Indians, and the Spanish state should, therefore, limit itself exclusively to its proselyting mission. The *Statement on the Damage and Injuries Done to the Indians* thus refutes the contention of another writer, Melchor Calderón, who defended the practice of enslaving natives in Chile as a way to end the permanent state of war among the Araucanians. In contrast to the Antilles, where Spanish institutions could take root right after the initial forays against the natives, the Spaniards encountered a series of customs and social organizations among the large Indian realms of Mexico and Peru that could not be broken up entirely lest warfare become chronic. Besides such jurists as Polo de Ondegardo and Juan de Matienzo among Viceroy Toledo's circle of advisors, there was Father José de Acosta, a theologian, historian, and keen interpreter of Indian affairs. His advice was certainly in Toledo's mind when he undertook to create an administration and a stable legal system after the long period of civil wars in Peru. To perceive the real nature of the natives, to ascertain to what extent it could be incorporated into colonial law, and what psychological and political factors must be taken into account when a Spanish organization was imposed upon the Peruvian masses—all this was the definite task of Polo de Ondegardo. His

Reports on the Serious Harm Resulting from Not Protecting the Tribal Rights of the Indians, his *The Errors and Superstitions of the Indians,* and his *The Lineage of the Incan Emperors* are interesting both as legal testimony and historical evidence. Similarly Matienzo, another member of Viceroy Toledo's retinue, made the first compilation of public law in the Indies in his *Government of Peru.*

Solórzano y Pereira's *Policy Concerning the Indies* (1648) is possibly the most outstanding work of baroque legal thought or, at any rate, it shares first rank with Antonio de León Pinelo's treatises on the interpretation of colonial law in the seventeenth century. In the ponderous prose of his commentaries, liberally sprinkled with classical quotations, Solórzano y Pereira seems the satisfied rhapsodist of the Spanish empire whose culture and proselyting mission allegedly justify its sovereignty in the New World. He points out that it was not simply the discovery and settlement which legalized Spain's dominion, but the fact that it had destroyed the idols and places of worship of the pagans, and that it had "forbidden them to eat human flesh, had abolished sodomy and incest, common vices in native societies, had prohibited their use of wine and moderated the consumption of *pulque,* and had overthrown the tyranny to which their chieftains had subjected them!" From the point of view of cultural history it is interesting to note how a Spaniard as eminent in the reign of Philip II as Solórzano y Pereira, could live in a closed world supremely convinced that the theological-legal ideas of the Spanish state were eternal and would never apply the critiques of contemporary European political science to these concepts. Solórzano y Pereira turned only to the writers of antiquity, the Church Fathers, and Spanish theologians for confirmation. His work provides the most sweeping panorama of New World institutions, from those of the natives (tributes, *encomiendas,* and workshops) to the organization of the Church and its relations to the state, city government (town councils, mayors), and the over-all political and legal entities such as the viceroyalties and the audiencias. In the final chapters of his voluminous work Solórzano discusses at length the mineral wealth of the colonies as he deals with their economic life. As a further expression of his medieval outlook he comments on the Thomistic theory of trade and financial profit in rigorously anticapitalistic terms.

The extensive writings of Antonio de León Pinelo—with their commentary on the Laws of the Indies, on the official acts and decrees of the Royal Council of the Indies, and on the royal confirmation of *encomienda* titles—have less stylistic and expository merit. This eldest offspring of the interesting and many-sided Pinelo family (Antonio, Diego, and John who all wrote on many different subjects) produced the first systematic American bibliography in his *Epitome of Eastern and Western Books* (1629). Because of his Semitic origin he wished, perhaps, as a government official and law commentator, to make patent his faithful devotion as a loyal vassal, but more than once his analytical vigor suggested the much-too-theoretical character of Spanish institutions in the Indies where laws were not always well adapted "to the local nature and situation." Another brother of this university-trained family, Diego, who was Protector of the Indians and Rector of the University of San Marcos, took note of a report by Juan de Padilla sent in 1660 to the viceroy of Peru, the Duke of Alba, listing in detail the abuses suffered by the native inhabitants. His *Reply* to this memorial hinted at a series of wise and benevolent administrative reforms designed to improve the lot of the aboriginal proletariat. *The Royal Treasury Report of Peru* (1647) by Gaspar de Escalona Agüero, which was both a report and a compilation of laws, dealt with analogous problems of labor, administration, justice, and the apportionment of tributes. Until Ulloa and Juan drew up their impressively precise report on economic and administrative conditions of the New World in the middle of the eighteenth century, *The Royal Treasury Report of Peru* was the economic historian's source for the operation of colonial institutions and the workings of the complicated fiscal scheme of the Spanish state in the southern colonies.

Historical writing of the baroque period differs from that of the sixteenth century not merely by its more ornate expression—the excessive rhetorical adornment of Spanish works such as Antonio de Solís's enormously popular *Conquest of Mexico*, for example—but also by its more limited and specialized range of subject matter.

Religious orders that had grown rich and were wrangling with each other over increased social control were now trying to write their own histories or those of their ecclesiastical districts. Among them are Dominican chronicles like Father Juan de Grijalva's on the establishments of his order in Mexico (1624), and Father Remesal's work (1619) on the activities of the same community in Chiapas and Guatemala. There were Franciscan chronicles about various districts in Mexico, such as Friar Alonso de la Rea's, a historian of Jalisco. Especially rich and diverse were the historical writings of the Jesuits whose economic power and spiritual influence exceeded every other relgious order in the sevententh century. In Peru the works of Buendía, Anello de Oliva, Manuel Rodríguez, and Samuel Fritz record the ups and downs of Jesuit expansion in the seventeenth century both in urban centers and towns and in the remote and dangerous missions that extended as far as the Upper Marañón river. In Mexico Father Francisco de Florencia's work appeared in 1624, long before Father Alegre wrote his celebrated *History of the Company of Jesus* toward the end of the eighteenth century and under the influence of the Enlightenment. The Jesuits were likewise creators of what might be called Paraguayan history and geography in a whole cycle of works, beginning with the previously mentioned *Spiritual Conquest* of Father Ruiz de Montoya and continuing with the writings of Fathers Nicolás de Techo, Lozano, and José Guevara. Foreigners such as the Austrians Dobriozhoffer and Pauke, the Englishman Thomas Falkner, and the Hungarian Ladislaus Orosz made their contributions to the problem of defining the obscure world of the Guaranís that Father Lozano had earlier described as a typical Jesuit conquest in which Spanish civil administration appeared to have no part. The regimented, socialistic Arcadia planted in the Paraguayan wilderness by the Jesuit fathers, the coöperative system of labor imposed on the Indians, and the peaceful, self-sufficient economic unit thus formed filled contemporary Europeans with the belief that it was the latest and most perfect version of Utopia. Even in the eighteenth century that inland region was undisturbed by the Antequera revolt, which was symbolically a conflict between the isolation and economic autonomy of the Jesuits and the centralizing effort of the viceroyalty. In all colonial Hispanic America, Paraguay remained its most tightly sealed area and its most theocratic community.

Two special histories of more literary appeal written in the baroque period were the *General History of the New Kingdom of Granada* by the Colombian Lucas Fernández Piedrahita (1688), and the *History of the Conquest and Settlement of Venezuela* by the Venezuelan José de Oviedo y Baños (1723). Both historians had the good taste to eschew baroque excess of ornate verbiage and tell their story with exceptional grace and ease. Bishop Piedrahita, who in his youth had written plays that were later lost, had a gift of lively narrative. Among the many interesting incidents of his life he tells how he won the friendship of the pirate Morgan. The latter, on one occasion, had offered him a pontifical tunic of the most elaborate workmanship, which he had stolen in Panama. It was the bishop's long contact with his fellowmen, perhaps, that equipped him with the narrative skill and the chatty manner that characterize his book. A rather idyllic poet, trained in the high company of Latin classical writers, was José de Oviedo y Baños, for whom colonial life at times seemed pleasantly pastoral despite the harsh realities of Spanish settlements in Venezuela. He was a delightful story teller even though it fell to him in his *History* to describe the cruel acts of an Ambrosio Alfinger or the diabolical deeds of the "Tyrant of the Andes," Aguirre. But he was at his best in such poetic episodes as the legend of Martín Tinajero, a soldier-saint of the conquest of Venezuela, who always shared his bread with the hungriest, who kept himself undefiled amidst the blood flowing about him, and who, when he died, willed his skull to the bees to make their honey in it. Oviedo y Baños wrote movingly and with grace on the rather ingenuous themes of saints' lives and the placid existence in early eighteenth-century Caracas with its many convents and gardens.

But there were other matters besides sketches of persons and places that engaged the historical writers of the time. They were still intrigued by the question of America's origin and its incorporation into European ideas, chronology, and theories concerning the world upon which Father José de Acosta had speculated so brilliantly.

When Sigüenza y Góngora studied the Aztec myth of Quetzalcoatl, he had tried to identify that legendary Mexican civilizer with the Apostle Saint Thomas whose journeys into mysterious regions were part of the Christian tradition. The supposition that the Indians had had some notion of Christianity before the arrival of the Spaniards turns up in other works, including the *Chronicle of Brazil* by the Portuguese Simon de Vasconcelos, and the *Spiritual Conquest of Paraguay* by Father Ruiz de Montoya. Whether Peru was the golden land of Ophir reached by King Solomon's ships, or whether the bridge between the Old and the New World was the lost continent of Atlantis that Plato referred to—these were the myths recurring again and again in the historical literature of the baroque age although José de Acosta had rejected them. Even at the close of the colonial period works still contained hypotheses as fanciful as the one in the Mexican Francisco Xavier Alejo Orrio's *Solution of the Great Problem of the Populating of America in Which, on the Basis of the Holy Books an Easy Route for the Migration of Men from One Continent to Another Is Learned* and Ordóñez y Aguiar's *History of the Creation of Heaven and Earth According to the System of Pagan America*. Orrio begins his book with an essay on a most intriguing world chronology. According to him, one thousand six hundred and fifty-six years elapsed between the creation of the world and the Flood. During that period the world was one, single, vast continent with mankind scattered all about it. A hundred and seventy years after the Flood one of Noah's grandsons, Misrain, who had possibly learned the art of observing the stars from his venerable grandfather, founded the kingdom of Egypt. After the great catastrophe of the Flood Noah lived for three hundred and fifty years and fathered innumerable sons and daughters who went about repopulating the world. The large island of Atlantis, to which Noah's ark had perhaps traveled, served as a way station between the Old and the New Worlds. Ordóñez's *History* is much more original than Orrio's book. The author, who was familiar with the Maya language and legends, attempted to connect some of these myths and the interpretation of the pictographs with the testimony of Biblical and Greek antiquity. In the popular mind of the time some Hellenic god, possibly Poseidon, who was always called by his Latin name Neptune, was the first settler on legendary Atlantis whence his descendants spread into the New World.

A more or less systematic study of the ancient codices and archaeological objects relating to the Maya and Aztec, which had begun in Mexico in Sigüenza y Góngora's time and more especially by Lorenzo de Boturini, stimulated eagerness in the eighteenth century to link indigenous legends and folklore with the Bible and classical mythology. America was to be explained not as some rare phenomenon or as a continent unknown before the arrival of the Spaniards but, rather, within the framework of universal history as set forth in the first book of Genesis. A similar association of the Old Testament with native myths was pursued in a strange work by Diego Bermúdez de Castro entitled *History of the City of Puebla* (1746).

But the end of the eighteenth century, as we shall see, brought a more rigorous interpretation, a clearer chronology, and a more rationalistic criticism to the facts of our Latin-American history, notably in the important works of Mexican Jesuits. The spirit of the Enlightenment, so perceptible in the rise of geographical studies and lengthy monographs on regions of America, brought new methods and new perspectives on the past.

Until critical attacks on scholasticism had throughly shaken the intellectual and spiritual foundations of colonial life, the physical image of the world in our baroque culture went little beyond what José de Acosta had stated in his classic work. A treatise on physics such as Father Elías del Carmen's previously mentioned, clearly shows what a student in Lima, Mexico City, Chuquisaca, and Córdoba was able to learn about the universe before the Encyclopedists had wrecked the intellectual and spiritual edifice reared during two centuries of Spanish domination. In America the eighteenth century was also to be a revolutionary era, and revolt in the minds of the people—"the crisis of the modern conscience," as Paul Hazard called it—that preceded political upheaval, just as it did in Europe. Benito de Gamarra's rebellion against scholasticism in Mexico by explaining Descartes and Leibnitz and his dismissal from his academic chair through conservative intrigue, or the accomplishments of Baltasar de los Reyes Marrero who suffered the same fate in Caracas, prove that a new age was dawning. This brings us to the problems and sensibility of the eighteenth century.

Eighteenth-Century
Jesuitic Humanism

FROM THE BAROQUE AGE TO THE EIGHTEENTH CENTURY

Until recently the standard, rather schematic, practice of Hispanic-American history-writing has presented the shift from the complex baroque period to the eighteenth-century revolutionary encyclopedism as an abrupt transition. It was alleged that toward the end of the seventeen hundreds a few brilliant minds suddenly emerged from the silent gloom of the colonies to give substance to new ideas charged with revolutionary ferment. According to this melodramatic concept of history the scholastic denizens of our medieval past were replaced, no one knows why or how, by these keenly satirical minds dangerously bent on change, such as Francisco Javier Eugenio Espejo, Miguel José Sanz, Antonio Nariño, Francisco de Miranda, Friar Servando Teresa de Mier, Manuel de Salas, or Mariano Moreno. These theoretical or practical rationalists were among those who paved the way to our Revolution for Independence. Even the soundest historians prefer to attribute the spread of revolutionary ideas to the eldest sons of wealthy Creole families who traveled to Europe and brought back, hidden in their ample baggage, the doctrines and writings that European rationalism was developing. One of these scholars was Miguel Luis Amunátegui who, in works that are still useful such as his *Precursors of the Independence of Chile*, or his

Chronicle of 1810, made a detailed study of the intellectual genesis of the separatist movement in his own country. This important cultural historian occupied himself at great length and with much documentation in writing about eighteenth-century secret gatherings such as those of José Antonio de Rojas in Santiago de Chile around 1780. The embryonic Chilean revolution of the three utopian Antonios— Berney, Gramusset, and Rojas—supposedly sprang from these meetings. In documents reminiscent of Rousseau they proclaimed the equality of all mankind and the necessity of creating states in America that would erase all differences of race or creed. Already it was the ideal of *egalité* that seemed to stir the Creole conscience most profoundly.

But if European influence was, indeed, injecting the virus of insurrection into the slothful body of the colonies from the eighteenth century on, it certainly did not achieve this end with the dramatic suddenness that these historians have alleged. Rather, one might say that the native organism itself was evolving a system of criticism of its own and slowly moving toward some distant utopia. Paul Hazard has traced the intellectual origins of the French Revolution back to the seventeenth century in his admirable *The Crisis of the European Conscience* and shown how much subversive criticism and how great an outcropping of new social and political values could be noted even in the majestic regime and rock-ribbed absolutism of Louis XIV. In the same way, our own newer ways of thinking did not spring up merely because a few bold Creoles traveled in Europe and brought back, like the Don José Antonio de Rojas in the sketch by Amunátegui, a load of banned books, or because some ship chandlers from Guipuzcoa carried the infectious germ of the Enlightenment to the Venezuelan coast according to the thesis attractively presented by the Spanish poet, Ramón de Basterra. These elements of imported culture were fruitful to the extent that they stimulated or helped to coagulate what was already beginning to take shape in that milieu. But there was no quick shift from scholastic theology to eighteenth-century ideology in our colonial universities. In forgotten theological tracts like the *Thesaurus Indicus* of the Peruvian Diego de Avendaño, for example, we have noted a theory of state that has affinities with the ideas of Locke and the Encyclo-pedists and a radically Christian concept of the social problems of America, such as Negro slavery. External as well as internal factors played a part in the evolution of our still insufficiently understood eighteenth century. Among the external influences were ideas of en-lightened despotism—French, English, and even Spanish in origin; the longstanding British policy of discrediting the Spanish empire in its American possessions; the preromantic Indianism of the time; and the extensive travel literature. Internal factors were the outgrowth of a more alert consciousness and the increased historical maturity of the Spanish Creole order.

JESUITIC POWER AND CULTURE

Jesuit humanism is one of the eighteenth-century bridges that joined the baroque age to the prerevolutionary period. A number of cir-cumstances determined the preëminence of the Company of Jesus among the religious communities established in the Indies. In the seventeenth century that order was the foremost cultural organiza-tion and one of the strongest economic and political forces in the whole colonial world. The international character of the Jesuits brought to their seminaries many remarkable foreign clergymen who, like Father Kino in the seventeenth century, were explorers and men of lifelong action or, like the Hungarians, Poles, and Germans, were earnest workers in the Paraguayan missions. Clearly the pres-ence of these foreign priests and friars introduced a new current of thought into the affairs of the Company and created a spirit dif-ferent from the traditionalism of the Spaniards.

Much research in geography and study of nature in Spanish Amer-ica were indebted to eighteenth-century Jesuit investigators. The great interest in natural history and pragmatic learning characteristic of the period is illustrated by such works as Father José Gumilla's *The Enlightened Orinoco* (1791), an excellent monograph on the Guianas that describes climatic phenomena, flora, fauna, and the ethnography of the interior; Father Vicente Maldonado's (1710–1744) *Chart of the Ecuadorean Territory*; and Father Juan de

Velasco's (1727–1792) *History of the Kingdom of Quito.* The new Jesuit pedagogy was to produce such works as the *Compendium of Geographical, Natural, and Civil History of the Kingdom of Chile,* and the *Essay on Natural History in Chile* by the Chilean Juan Ignacio Molina (1740–1829), published in exile, in which he describes that southern country with warmth and charm. Molina's work is a complete summary of things Chilean that was destined to become a source for the great nineteenth-century compilations of the natural history of that country by Claudio Gay and Domeyko. Indeed, well before the expeditions of Ruiz y Pavón and Mutis, and well before Humboldt appeared on the scene, this Chilean Jesuit had given a fascinating inventory of a Spanish American country to the cultivated world of Europe.

Added to the unmatched intellectual standards of the Jesuits in the eighteenth century were their economic power and formidable social influence. The wealth of the Order at that time derived from such varied properties as enormous plantations in the central valley of Chile, ranches in the River Plate region, large city and rural estates in Peru and Mexico, workshops in Paraguay, Peru, and Ecuador, and even mining interests in the Chocó area of New Granada. With the income from their vast holdings, the Jesuits directed and controlled seminaries and missions that enjoyed as much importance in the economic life of the colonies as the Order of the Templars did in Europe's Middle Ages. Jesuit seminaries and convents were not only the chief intellectual centers of small provincial towns of Hispanic America, Arequipa, Cuenca, Popoyán, Córdoba, and the like, but they provided the banking facilities and were inconspicuous forums in which local political problems were threshed out. Possibly this heavy involvement in American affairs and the broad, solid base of Jesuit operations explain why many of its members took a benevolent attitude toward the ideas of separatism and independence from Spain, which began to be bruited about in the eighteenth century. From this point of view the interests of the Order before its expulsion began to coincide with those of the regional bourgeois that considered its rise in the economic scale as handicapped by Spanish monopolistic practices and by the excessive, French-style centralization that the Bourbon dynasty was imposing. Long before the Jesuits were expelled, the conflict between the Order and the Spanish state over power and jurisdiction had steadily worsened, particularly in Paraguay where they held a veritable fiefdom. When the expulsion from Spain's domains in America finally came in 1767, a strong resentment against the monarchy inevitably arose among the Jesuits. This circumstance explains why Jesuit thought became bolder and more forthright in the abundant literature written in exile and why distinguished members or former members such as Vizcardo y Guzmán and Pozo y Sucre swung far over to what we would today call the revolutionary left by participating in the conspiracies to win independence fomented by Francisco de Miranda.

JESUITS AND THE EIGHTEENTH-CENTURY COLONIAL CRISIS

The work of outstanding Mexican Jesuits such as Francisco Xavier Clavijero, Francisco Xavier Alegre, Andrés Cavo, Andrés de Guevara, Pedro José Márquez, Manuel Fabri, Diego José Abad, and of the Guatemalan poet trained in Mexico, Rafael Landívar were of high intellectual caliber. Their writings indicate how near their ideas were to the concepts of social reform of the Encyclopedists without, however, losing sight of their own religious prepossessions. The best fruits of eighteenth-century Jesuit humanism were the writings of exiles who preferred Italian or Latin as their medium, thus making their works comparatively unknown to their Spanish American compatriots. To understand the sources of this humanism one must consider the common denominators of European thought which certainly influenced the Jesuits. To be remembered also are the specific data and exact information concerning America which they brought with them to Europe and the sharper edge that the perspective of distance gave to their knowledge. The unusual freedom of expression and the remarkable vigor on many pages of Alegre, Clavijero, or Guevara cannot be explained unless one is mindful of what was going on in the colonies, of the symptoms of discontent, and of the dawning nationalism that were stirring in the viceroyalties and captaincies-general. The fact that the Jesuits had lost their ascendancy in America, so that all that was left to them was to write and to die in a proper Christian manner, serves to underscore their noble effort to be truthful and their nearly always detached line of thought.

The seemingly firm edifice of the Catholic monarchy in the Indies, of which the Jesuits had been such effective custodians, was now beginning to shake. During the eighteenth century one local uprising followed another in the outlying provinces with periodical regularity. First came the Town Council's revolt at Asunción in Paraguay that turned into the Antequera revolution. Its populist slogans and heroic defense of local institutions against the centralizing tendencies of the monarchy caused a furor in both Buenos Aires and Peru. "The people's authority is superior to the king's," these commoners of Paraguay proclaimed. When the Peruvian viceroy's squad entered the central square of Lima to execute the rebellious judge Antequera, both the masses and the upper classes, united in an unwonted bond of fellowship by a vague hope of freedom and a better ideal of justice, hurled stones and, for the first time, raised subversive cries against royal authority. The blood of skirmishers of independence mingled with Antequera's. The memory of this famous commoner sank ever more deeply within the hearts of the people as his oft-told tale was repeated in songs and ballads despite the efforts of the viceregal police to suppress them. Historically Antequera came to represent the awakening of Spanish American political consciousness and the beginning of its attitude of open belligerence to the Spanish monarch.

Economic freedom, the end of the vicious system of military recruitment and ever-increasing taxes, the Indians' hatred for their Spanish magistrates, and a romantic hope of redemption were the excited watch cries with which the eighteenth century saw turbulent masses start in motion. In 1749 Juan Francisco León, followed by a mob of peasant workers and small cacao planters, would rise against the commercial monopoly of the Guipuzcoana Company in the wealthy provinces of Venezuela. The rebellions in the north of Argentina at La Rioja and Catamarca in 1752 were a protest against the arbitrary military conscription of the peasants. And never was the quiet existence of colonial life startled so much into a realization that there was an Indian problem, as in the eighteenth century. One of the many instances of the growing fear of the Spanish Court itself regarding the neglected Indian proletariat is the following secret order sent in April, 1782, by the sovereign to his viceroys at Peru and Buenos Aires:

> Many are the evils dominating the common run of Indians in the kingdoms of Peru and in the River Plate provinces, from which came the detestable practices that are forever tending to keep alive the memory of their pagan ancestors. The Indians are convinced that their connection and descent from their early pagan kings entitle them to be nobles and to call themselves Incas.

As a strange remedy for the bloody Indian uprisings the Spanish monarch decreed that the reading of the famous *Royal Commentaries of the Incas* by the Inca Garcilaso de la Vega should be banned in the Peruvian highlands since "the natives have learned much that is detrimental from it" and "thus the Indians will lack this cause for reviving their evil practices."

But the restlessness of the Indians resulted from something more than a fascination with their glorious, dead past. From 1749 to 1782, when the king signed this particular royal order, the colonies had witnessed large-scale uprisings and genuine warfare on the part of the Indian and mixed elements. Among these incidents were: a revolt of several chieftains in the vicinity of Lima and Huarochiri, Peru, in 1750; of Jacinto Canek who proclaimed himself king of the Mayas in Yucatán and, in 1765, stirred the Indian communities to rise against the collecting of tributes; and the fearful war in the Peruvian highlands from 1780 to 1781 in which Tupac Amaru's followers massacred Spanish magistrates, a small number of landowners, and lesser white officials of Indian villages. "The kings of Castile," declared Tupac Amaru, who proclaimed himself the avenging descendant of his Inca forbears, "have usurped my crown and the sovereignty of my people for three centuries by imposing upon my vassals an unbearable burden of tributes, imposts, tithes, excises, and taxes of every kind, along with tyrannical viceroys, judges, magistrates, and other officials who have treated the natives of this kingdom like beasts." These uprisings were put down and the death penalty was imposed on the leaders, in accordance with the still medieval concepts of Spanish justice. The limbs of the victims were scattered along the highways and their severed heads and hands were publicly exposed as a lesson to other so-called traitors. Despite this, the contagion of unrest was so strong and deep that revolt cropped up in other parts of the far-flung colonial empire. On the heels of the native insurrection in the Peruvian highlands came the equally desperate struggle of the commoners in New Granada who seized the funds of the royal treasury and tried to destroy the clumsy tribute-collecting mechanism that weighed so heavily on the small business and agricultural activities in the towns. A latent Indianism again made itself felt in the movement to obtain economic control, and in localities as far from Cuzco and the defunct Quechua empire as the Casanate plains bordering on Venezuela and the village of Silos situated on the eastern slope of the Colombian Andes the natives vowed support for Tupac Amaru and the restoration of the Inca state. During the last twenty years of the eighteenth century conspiracies among the intellectuals and the educated middle class paralleled the spontaneous movements of rural masses whose intuitive demand for reforms anticipated some of the issues that caused the nineteenth-century civil wars. These included a longing for social equality, protests against usurious money lenders and landed proprietors, resistance to imposts, and hatred for arbitrary conscription. The more cultivated elements—such men as Espejo in Ecuador, Nariño in New Granada, Rojas and Salas in Chile, and Gual and España in Venezuela—were beginning to sense that a time of profound change in history was imminent and that it was important to control events and profit by them.

Such a complicated social situation explains the tolerant attitude and the political audacity noted in the writings of the expelled Jesuits. Among them, a splendid group of Mexicans is conspicuous, because of their scientific and literary distinction. They present problems and ways of feeling and judging that were seldom apparent in the earlier works of colonial clergymen, in such books as the *Storia antica del Messico* by Francisco Xavier Clavijero (1731–1787), published in Cecena, Italy (1780–1781), the compilation of Andrés Cavo (1739–1802) translated as *Three Centuries of Mexico*, and *Elemental Philosophical Institutions* by Andrés de Guevara y Basoazábal (1748–1801). The ideas and style of these humanists reveal the endeavor to scrutinize the past and to seek approaches to a new kind of well-being or a new form of human justice. As we shall persently see, this encyclopedism with religious roots can be placed in importance beside secular revolutionary rationalism.

WRITINGS OF THE JESUIT EMIGRÉS.
THE MEXICAN HUMANISTS

Although the exiled Jeusits dealt with historical subjects, a kindred feeling, a common homesickness for the lost Eden of the Indies, and an identical attitude toward social and educational problems, seemed to bring unity to their pens. These writers felt themselves Mexicans far more than citizens of the Spanish empire that had punished and outraged them, and in a foreign sanctuary whose inhabitants knew so little about America, they endeavored to assert their nascent national pride and reveal to the educated world the wealth and the interest or fascination of their land of birth. Social reform and the theory of progress curiously inform the writings of this Jesuit group. They advocate a full-fledged policy of miscegenation to counter the bitter discontent of the many castes and the longing for equality so plainly evident in eighteenth-century thinking. Spanish America's future and social security depended upon a fusion of all racial elements to replace caste differences. Clavijero wrote: "There is no doubt at all that the policy of the Spaniards would have been wiser if, instead of fetching wives from Europe and slaves from Africa to Mexico, they had insisted upon making a single people out of themselves and the Mexican Indians." And Andrés Cavo in his *Three Centuries in Mexico* noted that the increasing ill will against the Spaniards in the colonies grew out of a justified feeling of racial rancor. Against the emotionally charged subjects of what might be called Spanish patriotism these same writers advanced an enthusiasm for the vindication of their own Indo-Spanish land. Many ancient forms of organization, social life, and native culture which the conquerors disdained or were unable to understand were so perfect, Clavijero noted, that "they alone would have sufficed to confound the haughty pride of those who believed that reason's empire was limited to Europe." The whole of his *Ancient History of Mexico*, which is like a broad, splendid statement in behalf of the aboriginal inhabitants, endeavors to prove, in the light of the new science of culture that was emerging in the eighteenth century, that the Indians had "souls fundamentally and, in every respect, similar to the souls of other children of Adam, that they were endowed with the same faculties," and that "the cultural level at which the Spaniards found the Mexicans was much higher than that of the Spaniards themselves when the Greeks, Romans, Gauls, Germans, and Bretons first came in contact with them." Moreover, even artistic creations and concepts of a more highly evolved civilization were present in the Indian societies. It is possible to express the strictest kind of Christian monotheism in the Mexican word *Teotl*, which Clavijero compares with the *Theos* of the Greeks. If, in approaching the Indians, the early missionaries and friars "had not been so excessively scrupulous and had imitated Saint Paul's example in Greece where he adopted the name Theos to designate far more abominable gods than those of the Mexicans and where he did not insist on requiring the Greeks to worship Him or the Adonai of the Hebrews," the pagans of America might have assimilated the Christian dogma far more readily. The Indian, it is fair to assume, would not have reacted to Christianity as an alien religion. That the Mexicans were far from being a barbarous people is likewise indicated by the richness and flexibility of a language such as Nahuatl which had "more augmentatives and diminutives than Italian, and it had more verbal and abstract nouns than English or any known tongue, for there was hardly a verb that did not form verbal substantives or an adjective that did not form an abstract noun." The well-known courtesy of the Mexicans which, among all the peoples of the hemisphere, is so characteristic of

Mexico, may possibly have come not merely from Spanish ceremonious ways but also from the nature of indigenous speech. The latter teems with particles "denoting respect which are added to nouns, verbs, prepositions, and adverbs." Other traits of the spoken medium are "variety, urbanity, and culture."

If the two major historians of the Mexican school, Clavijero and Andrés Cavo, tried to remove the erroneous concepts of the Europeans regarding the Indians and to bestow a universal character upon their indigenous qualities, another interesting Jesuit, Pedro José Márquez (1741–1820), who had mastered archaeology and art in Europe and was apparently influenced by the neoclassic esthetics of Lessing or Winckelmann, published, along with his treatise *On the Beautiful* and his *Escercitazioni Architettoniche*, an ingenious analysis of *Due Antichi Monumenti di Architettura Messicana*, enthusiastically dedicated "to the very noble, illustrious, and imperial City of Mexico." A sentence taken from this dedication suggests that what really mattered to him was not so much a separate description of monuments as his intention to incorporate into a more universal esthetic system forms of art that were so unlike the European. The history of art, then just beginning as a new discipline in the science of culture, set forth the urgency of devoting to Mexican monuments "an essay like those wanted in Europe." His fondest hope as an esthete and as a man deeply devoted to his country was to revive as far as possible the culture of the Indians which, according to Márquez, was ruthlessly destroyed by the Spaniards but deserved to be compared with the finest attainments of the Chaldeans, Assyrians, or Egyptians. The European world which, in condemning the native civilizations, spoke with horror of the human sacrifices of the Aztecs and branded them as barbaric, should remember that "almost no people in the world have not at some time practiced such rites. Even the Hebrews, despite their knowledge of the one true God, were occasionally guilty of the impiety of offering their sons to the idol of Moloch." And whoever views the pedestals of the Septimius Severus arch in proud Rome will note "carved in relief the unhappy slaves destined for the same kind of sacrifice. This rite differed from that of the Mexicans, of course, but both brought death to prisoners taken as slaves in war and were a form of homage to a divinity."

The thoroughly eighteenth-century idea of a universal culture rising above the prepossessions and differences of peoples and bringing the humanitarian concept into history, was enthusiastically commented on by Márquez and by his companion in exile and fellow clergyman, Andrés de Guevara y Basoazábal, author of *Elemental Philosophical Institutions*. Both were linked with the optimistic belief in progress which was so typical of the Enlightenment. From their lookout in Europe they felt that culture was reaching its moment of plenitude and that a world-wide understanding and synthesis above and beyond national groups and the provincialism of ancient history were desired. Those who fashioned these new values might be called "philosophers" who, according to Márquez,

> are cosmopolitan, consider all men as their compatriots, and know that any language, however exotic it may seem, may be as full of wisdom as Greek by virtue of its culture, and that any people may become as civilized as those who think that they are so in higher degree. In the matter of culture, philosophy does not recognize incapacity in any man, whether white or black, or whether educated at the poles or in the torrid zone. Granted the proper instruction, asserts philosophy, mankind in any climate has every potentiality.

Against authority and tradition Guevara y Basoazábal placed modern science in its dual aspects of rationalism and experimentalism. In a chapter of his book he enthusiastically praises Descartes, Galileo, and Bacon as the geniuses who pioneered the way to a new human culture. The man of the Enlightenment proclaims "reason as authority" in opposition to scholastic authoritarianism, and the "new truth takes precedence over moss-covered prejudice." Ever since Descartes, modern conscience "has cast off the yoke of slavery." The great problem of the moment is to spread the truth and the new methodology to the ever-growing masses and groups of mankind. Culture will be the agency, according to the thesis of both Jesuits, that will level differences, antagonisms, and feelings of inferiority among races and nations. Hence, with pathetic insistence, Guevara exhorts Mexican youth to study philosophy. It proves that "man was born for great and sublime enterprises." Consequently, America's backwardness with respect to imperial Europe is a transitory state readily overcome as the new knowledge spreads.

Another idea of the Enlightenment—the social contract and the democratic representative state in conflict with royal absolutism—is fully developed in the writings of the Jesuit Alegre. In quality and variety of subject matter his *Theological Institutions* and *Memoirs for the History of the Jesuits in New Spain* go far beyond what their titles imply. In the *Theological Institutions* things purely human are discussed as much as the divine. Starting from natural law and a broad background combining writings on modern politics, Greek philosophers, and Saint Thomas Aquinas, this Jesuit searches out and lays down the bases of a most benign Christian society. If, a century before, Bossuet had tried to draw the essentials of an aristocratic theory of the divine right of kings from the Holy Scriptures, Alegre proves that Christianity and representative government are not mutually exclusive terms. In an admirable discourse on the origin of authority the Jesuit argues that the latter does not derive from the intellectual or physical power of one who governs, nor that rulers receive it directly from God, nor that the pope can bestow it upon princes. The source and title to public power are none other than the consent of the community set forth in the social contract. With the awakened conscience of an American Creole, Father Alegre maintains that, in the conquest of America, acts of cruelty and needless mistakes were committed in the name of religion, that so unjustified a system as the slave trade disgraced life in its various regions, and that, in wishing to humble and reduce the native populations to a proletariat, a generous and practical utopian order like that of the great Bishop Vasco de Quiroga was allowed to fall into desuetude. Intellectually he is like one of the first representatives of modern religious thought who is no longer content with what is traditional and acceptable but wishes to bring within the orbit of Christianity the social and political feeling of his dynamic age.

NATIVIST ELEMENTS IN RAFAEL LANDÍVAR

Rafael Landívar's (1731–1793) *Rusticatio Mexicana* is the most sig-nificant purely literary work produced by the expatriate Jesuits. Out of this poem, which was rated by the Spanish critic Menéndez y Pelayo as one of the best in modern Latin, came rather paradoxically a cult of nativism in Spanish America and an idealization of rural life to which the Venezuelan Andrés Bello would contribute his celebrated *Silvas* a few decades later. Although Bello would give more extended treatment and the full eloquence of his neoclassical style to the theme of tropical agriculture and invite its development, and although his metaphors seemed to incorporate the plants and fruits of America into the polite verse of the time which the prevail-ing classical and mythological conventions had normally excluded until then, it is likely that the emotional response to nature is more freshly and immediately experienced in Landívar. He was an artist of exceptional visual richness who, although far away in Europe, never forgot the vivid outlines and light, the names and forms of things, or the minutest details of the Spanish American scene. Why, one asks, was such a delightful portrait of the countryside and its ways, in which the song of the quetzal bird competes with the sound of Indian oarsmen on Xochimilco or with the raucous uproar of a cock fight, written in Latin? Why was this work with its elements of a novel, its lyric charm, and its depiction of customs and man-ners thus limited to a small circle of readers? Perhaps it was a wan-derer's desire to communicate with European Jesuits for whom Latin was still the international medium. Or perhaps this contrast in con-tent and form of Landívar's nativist poem is explained by a purpose similar to what had moved Clavijero and Cavo to write their his-tories in non-Spanish languages, that is, as a demonstration of the cultural attainments of strangers in the land who had come from the far side of the Atlantic. Occupying an intermediate place in our literary history between the *Grandeur of Mexico City* by Bernardo de Balbuena, the best descriptive poem of the seventeenth century, and Bello's *Silvas*, which sang of the beauties of the tropical lands early in the nineteenth century, the *Rusticatio Mexicana* brought to a close the baroque cycle initiated by Balbuena, and it ushered in the more serene art of the great Venezuelan humanist expressed in his *Alocution to Poetry* and his *Song to Agriculture in the Torrid Zone*. While the fancy of Balbuena, an urban poet rather than a singer of rural scenes, senses an almost oriental exoticism in America, delights in its wealth and brilliance, and dwells on its gold, silver, and spices as symbols of its adventure-filled life and illusory dreams, the gentler tone and intimate details of Landívar's poem are an emanation of a fond association with its rustic customs and scenes. Despite a moralizing tendency in this eighteenth-century work and a certain didacticism, some of Landívar's cantos are reminiscent of a poet as ancient as Vergil and as modern as Pascoli, owing to the precision of natural detail and an understanding of the life of the humble. The Jesuit is charmed by the daily reality of the land far more than by the treasures of the Spanish galleons and by the mines of El Dorado which fascinated Balbuena. The latter confronted the "grandeur of Mexico" as if it were an unsolved mystery filled with the lure of adventure. Landívar's world was a more stable society that had already taken root in the valley of Mexico and in the green mountains of Guatemala. It was a society that bore the stamp of many generations that had performed the same tasks—a society that was beginning to ask of the land the why of its existence far more than for the elusive El Dorados. This poem was almost the first broad canvas in verse dealing with inhabitants and localities of the equatorial region, its alternating highlands and lowlands, its herds, plantations and farms, its colorful peasant festivities, language, and customs—all of which gave a unity to this Indian world stretching from the viceroyalty of Mexico to the viceroyalty of Peru. Distance made Landívar see the beauty of the lost world with the same vividness as it did the Inca Garcilaso de la Vega or Alonso de Ovalle who, in a sense, were his predecessors. The touch of nostalgia lends a lyric charm to the poem which might have been doubly tedious because it was written in Latin and because of its descriptive character. But the Jesuit knew how to handle with grace, color, and movement this new theme of the land that passed through

Andrés Bello to our own time in the *Manorial Poems* of Lugones. The fifteen parts of Landívar's poem offer an equal number of delightful frescoes of Spanish American life on the plantations: cowboys breaking in colts, native cloth and clay pottery piled up in village markets, Indians poling their *chinampas*, or floating gardens, feats on the *volador*, or lofty merry-go-round and on greased poles, and the orgy-like climaxes of cock fights. After the epics of the Conquest it is the Odyssey of the Indies, and it is one of the many paths leading to an awareness and conscious expression of what was native and indigenous. By a curious contradiction it is genuine Spanish Americanism in Latin. This effort of the Jesuit to put so many names and customs unknown to the classical world into the language of Vergil seems almost naïve. But, as was true of the writings of his fellow exiles, Landívar's poem is a living and breathing testimonial to an awakening nationalism that, nevertheless, does not conflict with the eighteenth-century aspiration for universal unity.

THE NEOCLASSICISM AND THE ZEAL FOR SECULAR LEARNING

Just about the time that the expatriate Jesuit poets and prose writers were composing their polished works with such marked urbanity, clarity, and regard for form, the neoclassic style, contrasting so sharply with baroque luxuriance, made its appearance in Spanish America. A new ideal of logic and precision replaced the tangled exuberance of baroque fashion. A wave of civic improvements appeared as a symbol of a time that was more secular than religious in the viceregal capitals, and even in the neglected captaincies-general that grew so rapidly in the second half of the eighteenth century. In Mexico City and Lima the boulevards, public buildings, fountains, and statues were absorbing some of the abundant wealth that formerly flowed into the monasteries and churches. More perceptible now was an ideal of a human culture that harmonized with the philosophy of the Enlightenment, one that no longer soared into the clouds of theology but, rather, tried to come to grips with more concrete matters like the problems of society, economics, and government. In Mexico City the College of Mining was built with the architectural proportions and geometrical measurements of a Renaissance palace. The Academy of Fine Arts was founded, which the great German scholar Humboldt was soon to admire. In Mexican cities two talented architects and sculptors, Tresguerras and Tolsá, would soon be satisfying the new urge for civic monuments and imposing architecture stirred by the spirit of a secular age. Now there was a transformation, a vital change in attitude and consciousness that inevitably affected the policies of progressive minded viceroys and governors such as Bucareli in Mexico, Guirior y Espeleta in New Granada, Vertiz in Buenos Aires, Ambrosio O'Higgins in Chile, and Centurión in the Venezuelan Guiana. These men looked past the circumscribed world of Spanish culture to the alluring ways of a cosmopolitanism more in harmony with the times, where money, economic realities, and labor were valued, and where a new upsurge of political freedom was felt. Wealthy Spanish Americans were traveling in Europe and returning home laden with banned books. An indication of the new laic tendencies were the social gatherings in cities where ideas were discussed and economic and educational reports were read. Also, fine music was performed at these meetings. For example, in Venezuela toward the end of the eighteenth century, José Ángel Lamas, Cayetano Carreño, Juan Francisco Velázquez, Caro de Boesi, and others represented the most remarkable flowering of musical talent anywhere in the colonies. The stirring notes of the great European music by Scarlatti, Hadyn, and Mozart were heard in the Caribbean highlands.

Learning had acquired a secular garb among the thinkers and dreamers of the closing years of the eighteenth century. At that time the two large capitals, Mexico City and Lima, that previously had monopolized the wealth and culture of the Indies, were challenged by other cities, which were rising in importance because of the relaxation of trade restrictions and the exportation overseas of food products. Thus, Caracas and Buenos Aires became centers of insurrection against the mother country; Santa Fe de Bogotá cultivated a group of scholars around Mutis, Caldas, and Nariño; and Havana organized the first Economic Society of Friends of the Country. It was a time when the dream of a better future and of greater human happiness inspired two types of human reaction. On the one hand was the serious, rationalistic deviser of systems who believed that the human mind had the gift of learning from the experience of the past and could attack the problems of the future with wise measures; on the other was the sentimentalist who believed that, once mankind was freed from the oppressive errors and prejudices of age-long tyranny, a fountain of infinite goodness would gush forth from its own heart. At this moment of the eighteenth century, rationalism and a Rousseau-like feeling worked together to bring about a common utopia of progress. Confronted by innovation and reform, the tide of conservatism ebbed steadily away. Even the Spanish state, an air-tight compartment in the seventeenth century, had succumbed to French influences in the eighteenth. Interestingly enough, the restlessness of the colonies was oddly reflecting the flow of ideas in Spain. There encyclopedic learning and the acceptance of experimental science first cropped up in Feijóo's essays. The lay state and political realism in its modern form were implicit in the schemes of the Count of Aranda; the new science of economics was discernible in the ideas of Campomanes and Jovellanos, and the standards of neoclassic literature, with its grammatical and logical precision and even its prosy didacticism, were plainly visible in the writers of the time from Iriarte to Moratín. Is it not strange then that, just on the eve of drastic changes in political and social values, the ideas of the Spanish American Jesuits should seem so modern to us and that they should coincide, to some extent, with the reality of the lay world of their time? Revolutionary tendencies were on the march and the moment had not yet arrived when a new dialectic of conservative thought could be shaped to confront them.

Eve of the Revolution

COSMOPOLITAN AND HUMANISTIC IDEALS OF THE ERA

Two kinds of cosmopolities generated the state of mind or attitude usually called "Encyclopedism" or the "Enlightenment." First, the European who, no longer content with his traditional way of life and impelled by intellectual curiosity or by mere restlessness, traveled to distant lands to compare his age-long values with those of newer peoples whom he had scorned or underestimated until then. Second, the American-born Spaniard who felt uncomfortable in the isolation of his narrow colonial world and wished to acquire the ideas and practices of the older Europe. These two types furnished some of the ingredients that conditioned the mind and thought of eighteenth-century Hispanic America. The Counter Reformation and the baroque age had accentuated the religious and national differences of nations and had erected barriers of suspicion between countries, but the new era was internationally oriented. The world seemed to be shrinking and there was a desire to melt all knowledge of races and peoples into one science of humanity. Eighteenth-century man wanted both depth and breadth of information. He yearned to make clear through a systematized rationalism not only what a Frenchman was or a Spaniard, but also what he was himself. Besides, he longed to beautify the ageing garden of European culture with the exotic plants of other civilizations. The men of the eighteenth century appreciated Chinese vases and Japanese art along with

147

the mosaics of Pompeii. At the same time, a *mal de siècle* weariness moved them to deny the ancient values of European culture and to seek, like Rousseau, an ingenuous world of unspoiled places beyond the seas. This preromanticism of the eighteenth century had a special significance for Hispanic America by bringing Indianism into fashion and the indigenous elements into competition with those of the dominant Spaniard. On reading *The Incas* by Marmontel, and the *History of European Settlements in the Indies* by Abbot Raynal even a person as cosmopolitan as Francisco de Miranda toyed with the idea, in his earlier hopes and dreams of independence, that newly established states in the Western Hemisphere might restore an Incan realm, using the Spanish language as its medium.

As a base for his nationalistic reasoning the American-born Spaniard could point to a rich assortment of descriptive and critical writings inspired by his America. They had grown from the age's scientific curiosity and also from propaganda against Spain concocted in France and, more especially, in England which country was eager to have access to the overseas routes and markets of the tottering Spanish empire. Along with contraband goods the colonists received banned books and arguments to support their growing subversion. What smugglers failed to bring, the Creoles of Spanish America got for themselves in the cities and capitals of Europe. The easiest areas for contraband activities were along the Venezuelan coast because of its proximity to the English, French, and Dutch Antilles, and ideas could slip through to the mainland just as well. In the last third of the eighteenth century educated men and conspirators of the stature of Pablo de Olavide and Francisco de Miranda had been living in Europe where they had succeeded in working their way into the most exclusive aristocratic and revolutionary circles. The secret societies, that were so typical of the preromantic era, with their lure of clandestine rites, dark chambers, and special oaths, provided these utopian dreamers and gifted adventurers with a kind of liturgical passport that enabled them to pass from one country to another. A republic had been created in the United States and personalities such as Franklin and Jefferson made it seem to the opponents of absolutism a promised land of "virtue" and "happiness." Even in the Spanish colonial world ideas were beginning to reach the man in the street. Debates and discussions featured the various social gatherings of an incipient middle class, of high officials vaguely imbued with rationalistic concepts, and of youthful heirs of entailed estates who had returned from Europe. Talk of this sort had its effect on the lucid and didactic prose of the early gazettes and periodicals. This contagion of thought also emanated from the Spain of Charles III. The Societies of Friends of the Country, which had been organized in Spain since 1785 "to improve the popular arts and crafts and to facilitate and aid their use and instruction" were beginning to spring up in Spanish America. One appeared in Quito in 1792 and another in Havana a year later. These institutions were orienting the Creole mentality toward more definite and practical goals.

By royal decrees the enlightened despotism of Charles III had endeavored to sweep away the lingering remnants of a decadent scholasticism still infesting Spanish pedagogy. He urged the University of Alcalá "to reduce to a proper limit the verbalistic subtleties of that kind of learning" and to pay more attention in their curricula to Feijóo's methods. These circumstances had stimulated openly antischolastic instruction in colonial lecture halls on the part of such men as Díaz de Gamarra in Mexico, and Baltasar Marrero in Caracas, and they had brought on the famous conflict over the rectorship at the University of San Marcos in Lima in 1783 when the younger men backed the candidacy of the rationalistic José Baquíjano y Carrillo against the tradition-bound contestant. In these closing years of the century colonial life, for the first time, experienced a high degree of tension, a sharply drawn clash of ideas, and a painful conflict between generations.

The incipient insurgency in the air was conditioned, to be sure, by more pressing and immediate factors as, for example, the rising importance of the wealthy Creole proprietors in the second half of the eighteenth century. No longer were their economic aspirations satisfied by the Free Trade Regulations of 1778, for they now wished to deal with every nation unhampered by any restrictions. To Spanish Americans the Peninsular official was an annoyance, and they longed to add political authority to economic power. The whole eighteenth century witnessed resentment, surreptitious rebellion, and hatred on the part of these Creole landowners who were coming into the fullest realization of their own importance just at the time that the Bourbon monarchy was most energetically striving to impose its highly centralized administrative and fiscal system upon the colonies.

Unlike the treasure seekers of the Conquest and the lucky miners of the seventeenth century, the planters of the eighteenth century felt a deep sense of belonging to the land. Far more keenly they felt the irritation of the American-born toward Peninsular Spaniards and, as leaders with a substantial following, they fought for their right to prevail in the town councils. The spark of insurgency ignited most violently in purely agrarian countries such as Argentina, Venezuela, and Chile that had achieved a large degree of prosperity in the second part of the century—larger indeed than the wealthy viceroyalties of Mexico and Peru that were centers of the old mining economy and were more closely affiliated with Spain through a bureaucratic mechanism and a powerful aristocracy. In the newer parts of the colonial empire the American-born elements did not run into the wall of an upper class so tightly bound to the monarchy as in Peru and Mexico, nor did they contend with the dead weight of a long established administration bolstered by the passive attitude and wretchedness of huge Indian masses.

If every period fashions its own human archetype—an archetype that embodies its passions and its ways of seeing and feeling—it may be said that, in the most representative Creoles of this era, such as Miranda, Francisco Javier Eugenio Espejo, and Caldas, restlessness and an active, satirical discontent were the common intellectual and spiritual symptoms beyond individual differences. In the emerging dream of a free and prosperous Spanish America the mordant sarcasm by which the old ways were assailed was similar in effect to the enthusiasm with which the newest utopian ideas were hailed. A passionate fervor regarding the future and a caustic condemnation of the past existed side by side in individuals of such rich, if at times contradictory, lives as those of the precursors of our independence.

Having come down from the airy heights of theology, the man of the Enlightenment now sought a better control and utilization of earthly things. His occasionally pedantic eagerness for change, coupled with a blind faith in the ethical and social value of science, contained the seed of nineteenth-century industrialism.

Did not Curtius say that what characterized rationalist thought—whence would come the dialectics of our Revolution—was its abandonment of abstraction and its aim to arrange knowledge about the world so as to facilitate political freedom and blue print new social ways? In Spain such writers as Jovellanos, who had composed tragedies, were not above writing about agriculture, commerce, public philanthropy, or transportation. This is what gave the eighteenth century its prosy dullness but also its practical effectiveness. There are many worlds and cultures besides the Spanish, declared a Creole of the Enlightenment with an almost unjustified contempt for his own heritage. An eagerness for novelty, even for foreign imitations, had supplanted the proud self-sufficiency, the medieval concepts of honor, and the haughty disdain for everything alien that had characterized the Hispanic culture of the baroque age. Travel and modern languages were indispensable elements in the education of the time. The youthful soldier Francisco de Miranda, whose early restlessness drew him from the pleasant valley of Caracas to Spanish barracks in Africa, Florida, and Cuba, and to a dangerous intimacy with English officers and administrators at Jamaica, found it expedient to take leave of his benefactor, Cacigal, in order to elude the police who were beginning to get on his trail. As he prepared for his journey to the United States, he set down in a letter what might be regarded as the ideal of a restless Creole in 1783. He wrote Cacigal that he was leaving

> to begin his travels in foreign parts. With this purpose in mind, I have carefully cultivated beforehand the leading European languages. That was the profession for which fate and birth have destined me from my earliest years. All these beginnings, for so far that is all they are, all these seeds which, with no little labor and cost, I have been planting in my mind during my thirty years, would of course be fruitless and unprofitable with-

out the experience and knowledge that one acquires by visiting in person and assiduously examining the great book of the universe. This means its wisest and most virtuous societies, their laws, government, agriculture, civilized ways, military science, navigation, arts and crafts, and the like. This and this alone can ripen the fruit and complete, in some degree, the great task of creating a man of solid worth.

Does not this youthful letter of Miranda express every single one of the drives, and even the banalities, of the age of the Enlightenment, that is, the desire to travel and see, to replace the former criterion of authority by direct observation, and the inclusion also of the romantic allusion to the "great book of Nature"? This talented conspirator was completely in tune with his time—he noted down at great length everything he saw, studied, or learned in the museums of Italy and Germany, at the banquets and hunting parties in the Russian Court, and even how much he paid a courtesan in Rome. All this he managed to record in documents still preserved among his papers while engaged in stealthy, long-drawn-out intrigues against the Spanish empire, organizing secret societies, offering plans to the British Foreign Office, sending agents and spreading propaganda from Mexico at one end of the continent to Buenos Aires at the other end. A greedy desire for knowledge and a certain crass materialism, which in no way conflicted with his revolutionary zeal and his courtly manners of a perfect gentleman, were an expression of the typical complexity of the age.

Still another facet of this omnipresent restlessness was his mocking satire and corrosive commentary on things colonial in general. Every period of social change and of a break in tradition is preceded by waves of sardonic humor and satire. The Middle Ages expired in the varied manifestations of "the dance of death," in Villon's poems, and in the irreverence of Italian story tellers, much as the age of absolutism dissolved in the irony of Voltaire and of the *Persian Letters*. Our eighteenth-century literature, which was the expression, of course, of a far less mature milieu, offers no such glorious examples, but it did produce instances of a tart and biting humor in writings such as Concolorcorvo's *Guide of Blind Travelers*, some of Francisco

Javier Eugenio Espejo's pages, Simón de Ayanque's (Esteban de Terralla's) *Lima Inside and Out*, and even in Friar Servando Teresa de Mier's deliberately polemical sermons, particularly the one preached in 1794 at the Feast of the Virgin of Guadalupe, which launched this subversive curate's turbulent career.

When the pseudonymous Concolorcorvo—whose name was Calixto Bustamante Carlos Inca—declared that, as a person of mixed blood, he could expect no better appointment than that of "dog catcher" of the Cuzco cathedral, and when a man of part Indian and Mulatto blood like the highly intelligent native of Quito, Espejo, stated that he owed his nobility solely to himself, both were assailing the foundations of privilege and social inequality upon which the whole colonial structure rested. A society in crisis composed of varied and conflicting human species and depicted with irony, color, and sarcasm, emerges from Concolorcorvo's wanderings through the Argentine plains to the Peruvian highlands, and from the panorama of the streets, squares, and balconies of Lima in which the picaresque Terralla whiled away his time. Types included were the bishop and magistrate, the priest of the Indian villages who knows how to swing the incenser and manage religious processions, shyster lawyers, procurers, and go-betweens. Burnished glints of satirical detail on customs and manners occasionally sparkle even in the learned and bureaucratic prose of the well-known *Secret News of America* by the travelers Juan and Ulloa. And many years later the scientific-minded Caldas, who founded the *New Kingdom of Granada Weekly* as a vehicle for statistical information, descriptions of natural resources and useful products of the viceroyalty, meteorological data, and suggestions about agriculture and the crafts, would vary his clear, didactic style by pages of sharp social criticism. Discussing the Ecuadorean city of Cuenca in volume 111 of the *Weekly*, for example, the geographer and botanist in him yields to the sociologist and critic of customs who writes with luminous and pitiless realism. Caldas's blunt pages contain searing passages on the injustice, indeed the ridiculousness, of a society composed of an idle aristocracy that lives off the land that it poorly cultivates, indulges in litigation and petty disputes over honor and hierarchy, while its tawdry and tarnished blazonry bends the backs of the humiliated elements of mixed blood who performed almost all useful labor, and crushed the hapless Indian, victim of the "harshness of masters and priests." The pristine values of this Spanish American world had deteriorated or become wholly unresponsive to the needs of changing times. Spanish pride had turned into sheer vainglory, honor was a mask of slothfulness, and religion was more empty liturgy than feeling, a fustian cloak of ignorance and superstition.

The clamor for change, for colonial life to come abreast of the fast moving reforms sweeping Europe and, since 1776, the United States arose not only from famous conspirators and travelers such as Miranda and Olavide, those knight errants of the Enlightenment, but also from the new generation of academicians, utopian thinkers, and philanthropists that had appeared in Spanish American cities. These were men of the type of José Antonio de Rojas or Manuel de Salas in Chile, Belgrano in Buenos Aires, and Licentiate Sanz in Caracas. Was it not true that a gifted statesman within the monarchy itself, the Count of Aranda, had grasped the urgency of radical reform to head off the possible disintegration of the empire? The prophecies contained in his 1783 memorial were an anticipation of history. There he predicted what the influence of the independence of the United States, which Spain had helped to achieve, would be on the Spanish American colonies. He foretold the tremendous stimulus that the new English-speaking state, inexorably destined to become a rival, would give to the new ideas of political and economic freedom against which the old regime in Spain would vainly struggle. To save Spanish possessions overseas Aranda proposed a Hispanic Commonwealth similar to what the British later organized in the twentieth century. Concerning the future of the thirteen colonies liberated by Washington and destined to become the mighty United States he declared:

> That Republic was born a pigmy, so to speak, and it required the help and support of two nations as powerful as France and Spain to win its independence, but the day will come when it will be a giant, a veritable colossus of awe-inspiring dimensions in that part of the world, and then, forgetting the benefits re-

ceived, it will think only of its own interest and aggrandizement. Freedom of conscience and the abundance of fertile land in which to settle and develop a vast population, together with the special advantages conferred by its recently established government, will surely bring to its shores the craftsmen and farmers of every nation.

To carry out so bold a scheme as Aranda's—to create in Spanish America a confederation of three great states under Spain's sovereignty—the Bourbon dynasty would have needed a great king and a large body of men of Aranda's lofty intellectual caliber. Unhappily, after the reform movement of Charles III, the Spanish state relapsed into the control of the "kitchen cabinet" of the mediocre Charles IV. The French Revolution, Napoleon's vast adventures, and the commercial and naval preponderance of England shifted world history into other channels. Aranda, the most significant statesman that Spain had produced since the days of Cardinal Cisneros, remains as one of those clear-sighted observers of a historical reality that tragically eluded his control and superb human qualities.

Let us pause to consider the most important impulses in eighteenth-century Spanish colonial thought that effected a revolution in its spirit several decades before armed revolt broke out.

THE "BOOK OF NATURE." ENCYCLOPEDISM IN NATURAL HISTORY

A leitmotiv of the time was the "book of Nature" that Miranda had mentioned in his letter to Cacigal. The growing interest of European countries, notably England and France, in assuring the freedom of the seas for their own international trade together with the spirit of research in natural history characteristic of the age, made the eighteenth century a period of scientific expeditions and of voyages bent on clearing up the confused cartography of distant shores and countries, determining their latitudes astronomically and, at the same time, making botanical and zoölogical studies of overseas areas. Commercial and political advantage was thus identified with scientific curiosity. Some of these eighteenth-century travelers,

Louis de Bougainville for instance, cleverly combined a scrutiny of nature with adventure and brought back information of interest to both their monarchs and their academies of science. With specimens from so many distant places, botanical gardens, mineralogical collections, and museums of "curiosities" were established in European capitals from Madrid to Saint Petersburg. The enlightened despots also became royal collectors. For colonial Spanish America the voyages were especially useful both because they made the knowledge of its own geography more exact and because they served as a reagent of new kinds of thinking, methods, and observations to teach the Creole to know himself and the world about him. The traveler of that age was not a dry specialist content to draw maps or determine the position of stars; rather, he provided his readers with a narrative full of picturesque details concerning the remote communities that he had visited. A rich travel literature appeared throughout the century, and Frenchmen and Englishmen, from Frezier in 1713 to Vancouver in 1795, who skirted the shores of America, were the forerunners of the great Alexander von Humboldt through whom its geography, and even its sociology, would reach scientific maturity. These descriptive writings supplied material for a new vision of Spanish American life and for a critical evaluation of the Spanish colonial system that was useful both for scientific purposes and the national interests of the authors. They also provided arguments that the Creoles later used against the mother country, that is, its religious fanaticism, administrative abuses, cultural backwardness, and the need to redeem the Indian. The foreign traveler inevitably looked at things through his own prejudices or through the myths of his own people. In this way, around 1713, Frezier described, with Voltairian mockery, the Church's influence in Chile, the shallow ostentation of its ecclesiastical ceremonies, the decadent euphuism of the priests' sermons, and the blind reverence demanded of the masses. Forty-odd years later when Commander Byron was shipwrecked on the island of Chiloé he viewed the quaint customs of that remote corner of America with the eye and the feelings of a reader of Rousseau. Almost as if he were anticipating the poetry of his grandson, Lord Byron, he depicted a romantic scene wherein the lovely niece of the village curate, stricken with love for an English sailor, opened an ancient colonial chest in which she kept her party dress and her earrings and pendants, and seemingly sought to lure the lad both by her fresh beauty and by her small, rustic treasures. And the Commander, full of the feeling of the age, contrasts the stiff formality and conventions of European life with the Acadian simplicity of existence in that out-of-the-way corner of America. He liked to think of life there as a sentimental tale that resembled Bernardin de Saint Pierre's *Paul and Virginia* even down to its harrowing shipwreck. There were the "green hills, the sea, and the simple and virtuous inhabitants" just as in the good abbot's story.

As if to emulate the examples of France and England, eighteenth-century Spain organized its own scientific expeditions. Among the members of the commission formed by Charles de La Condamine and other French savants to locate exactly the equator in Ecuador were the distinguished Spaniards Jorge Juan and Antonio de Ulloa, whose many nautical, geographical, and social observations were to be recorded in their two famous books, *An Historical Account of a Voyage to South America* and the almost revolutionary *Secret News*. The presence of these foreign scientists in Quito undoubtedly inspired the work of earnest scholars there. Such were Judge Dionisio de Alcedo, who gathered the documents for a detailed survey of the continent later so useful to his son, Antonio de Alcedo, author of the first large *Historico-Geographical Dictionary of the American Indies*, published thirty years later (1786–1789) in Madrid, and the learned Pedro Vicente Maldonado (1710–1748), who went to Europe with La Condamine to show his topographical maps and tables of measurement compiled in Ecuador and who was presented to the academies of science in Paris and London by the celebrated Frenchman. In Lima members of the expedition met José Eusebio del Llano Zapata, probably the best mathematical mind in the continent at the time, who was at work on his ambitious project, the *Historical, Physical, and Apologetic Memoirs on South America*. This effort marked an enormous advance over the earlier writings of Peralta Barnuevo and Sigüenza y Góngora. It was men of the caliber of Maldonado, Llano Zapata, and the remarkable Mexican astronomer and mathematician Joaquín Velázquez de Cárdenas who, in the fifth decade of the eighteenth century, symbolized the new and more precise attitude that directly opposed clarity and method to the fustian erudition of the baroque age. It was during the rule of Charles III, however, that the great feat of describing and classifying the phenomena of Spanish America got most impressively under way with the expeditions sent to Mexico under Martín de Sessé, to Peru and Chile under Ruiz y Pavón, and to New Granada under José Celestino Mutis. Their reports and drawings of specimens of Spanish American botany, zoölogy, and their descriptions of climatology, many still unpublished in the archives and museums of Madrid, offer eloquent testimony to this enthusiastic but short-lived moment of Spanish science.

Not every distinguished traveler returned to the Spanish capital. The famous Mutis stayed at Bogotá where he trained an able generation of naturalists and scholars who later published the meaty *New Granada Weekly* under the editorship of Caldas. The celebrated Czech mineralogist Tadeo Haenke remained in Peru where he died a forgotten resident of Cochabamba in the days of the independence movement. When Humboldt came to Mexico at the beginning of the nineteenth century he admired the new scientific rationalism flourishing in its national institutions such as the School of Mines and their teachers such as Antonio de León y Gama (1735–1802) and Andrés del Río, the discoverer of vanadium and the earliest translator of Lavoisier's *Chemistry* into Spanish. At the same time science was progressing in Peru in a straight line from the *Almanacs*, in which the cosmographer Cosme Bueno published his statistical and meteorological reports about that viceroyalty, to Ruiz y Pavón's *Flora Peruviana et Chilensis*. Science reached a climax toward the end of the century in the bold and most rigorously modern scientific thought represented by Toribio Rodríguez de Mendoza and especially by Hipólito Unanue. The latter, like Caldas, was one of the Spanish Americans with the most universal scientific outlook that the declining days of the empire produced. He combined the qualities of a close observer of nature and of an ardent interpreter of social phenomena much after the manner of Caldas. His very original

Observations on the Climate of Lima, which closely approached modern concepts of human geography, endeavored to determine the relations between man and his environment. A reader of Montesquieu, he puzzled over why social psychology was conditioned by surroundings. And since this meteorologist-physician had also read Rousseau, he trumpeted "back to nature" and plenty of fresh air as the most effective therapeutics against illness and as the basis of a new educational system. For Unanue the word "oxygen," that Priestley had used for the first time to define a component of the air, had the fascination of a miracle. Nature was far more than a subject for study in those preromantic days; it was the starting point of a new religion, and nature was the mother of instinct whom one invoked in the now open rebellion against the older way of thinking with its prejudices and repressions.

To spread natural and social sciences among the population a curious kind of journalism flourished at the close of the eighteenth century. The "random sheets," "announcements," and "reports of events" available at infrequent intervals in the seventeenth century were followed in the eighteenth century by more learned periodicals dealing with "various matters relating to the sciences and arts," as the Mexican natural scientist, Antonio Alzate, phrased it in his publication appearing in 1772. Running through these series of media, from the *Mexico City Gazette* to the openly insurgent journals appearing at the outset of the war for separation such as the *Buenos Aires Gazette,* the *Caracas Gazette,* or the *Aurora of Chile* (1808–1810), one can trace for almost ninety years the complex and excited advance of Spanish American consciousness as it groped its way toward political freedom. As one reads in these papers, of which the *Peruvian Mercury,* the *Periodical Paper of Bogotá,* the *Periodical Paper of Havana,* and the *New Kingdom of Granada Weekly* are especially noteworthy, one can measure day by day and from capital to capital how the alluring utopias elaborated in the eighteenth century were registering increasingly on the Creole mind. Fearful of the possible effects on the native mentality of a dangerous journalism that was so avid for new ideas, Matías Gálvez, Viceroy of Mexico, wrote in 1784:

I consider the *Gazette* very useful provided it confines itself to small matters, that is, to arrivals and departures and cargoes of ships and natural products, to the appointments of prelates and magistrates, assumption of office by church canons, and other newsworthy details of this kind that are a part of the daily life of so large an area. All this sort of thing is soon forgotten but, among a lot of trivial nonsense that is inevitable in every publication of this nature, these gazettes could be a means of preserving public events that are soon forgotten but well to record.

Then he added: "Moreover, it is important to provide harmless matter to satisfy the public's curiosity."

But studious and insatiable readers were no longer content with the "harmless" items that the viceroy referred to. Now they wanted to change the social order and the cultural ideas of their own contemporaries. With detailed documentation the Argentine scholar José Torre Revello has told the story of the ups and downs of this colonial journalism, and there is no point in repeating his exhaustive account. What is important in this brief treatment of our "Enlightenment" is the representative type of journalist-man of science, men like Caldas, Unanue, or Espejo who, by means of the gazettes, got in touch with like-minded persons scattered over the chief cities and towns of Spanish America. They were the ones who supplied the data for a new concept of the world drawn from the currents of European social and scientific thought. They were brushing aside the verbal cobwebs and fanciful superstitions that had hidden from the Creole a real knowledge of his environment and of his fellow beings. And they were beginning to get down to the bedrock of the reality of America. "Useful plants," variety of climates and regions, how crafts could be improved, or how outworn methods of instruction could be bettered were subjects that claimed their attention. The driving force behind these journalistic endeavors were the ideas of social utility, philanthropy, and exploitation of nature deriving from the rationalism of the time. The word "progress" with all its illusions and hopes for the future was emblazoned on the editorial pages of the gazettes. The men who wrote these learned "memorials" were not solitary thinkers but determined men of action, like Belgrano, Manuel de Salas, Espejo, Caldas, and Nariño. They strove to set up technical schools, encourage economic associations, and build hospitals, theaters, or pawnshops. It is exciting to hear a man like Caldas—and one feels he is actually talking—urging the citizens of Tunja, Ibagué, Pore, or Popayán—tiny communities lost in the lonely immensity of the viceroyalty of New Granada—to send in local news, vital statistics, and descriptions of plants peculiar to the vicinity and their methods of cultivation. Everything is collected in the pages of the weekly with the same spirit of public service, from the important works of the distinguished naturalist himself such as his *State of Geography of the Viceroyalty with Relation to Its Economy and Commerce* or *The Influence of the Climate on Organic Beings*, to the statistical reports of the cities and towns. Mutis's great disciple brought together a corps of collaborators for the important task of a scientific study of his country. It included Joaquín Camacho, Mariano del Campo, Benedicto Domínguez, Jorge Tadeo Lozano, and others. An important item of news in the pages of the periodical was the announcement that a young chemist and mineralogist by the name of José María Cabral had arrived in the inland city of Bogotá and that, at the request of the editor of the *New Kingdom of Granada Weekly*, he had agreed to analyze free of charge any mineral samples that were sent to him. "Surrounded as we are by emeralds, amethysts, cinnabar, platinum ore, iron, copper, and lead," wrote Caldas in his notice, "and literally treading on gold and silver, we are poverty-stricken in the midst of riches because we do not know our own property. It is essential to know how to distinguish and recognize the worth and advantages that we could derive from nature's bounty in these favored lands."

What is demanded of the new kind of learning and what is the archetype of savant and reformer needed by Spanish America according to Caldas' thinking? He answered these questions in an admirable eulogy of a distinguished Ecuadorean, Pedro Vicente Maldonado, who died prematurely. He must be "a man of genius distinguished in learning above all his fellow countrymen, he must travel into every corner of his country, break new paths, sail its waters, observe, and measure; he must make copies of books, sketches, and instruments; and he will try to acclimate the arts and sciences in his native land." This dynamic concept of culture and of the intellectual eager to convert ideas into facts was an entirely new contribution of the collaborators of the gazettes to the hitherto static background of colonial society.

THE STUDY OF SOCIETY. THEORY OF A
NEW EDUCATION

The study of society was a logical transition from the study of nature. It was desirable to transfer the methods of measurement and analysis from the natural sciences to social phenomena with the same kind of exactness. In contrast to the artificiality of baroque thought with its resort to the abstract, the decorative, and the verbalistic, thinking was now for the first time in terms of a pitiless realism. The social criticism of our writers at the close of the eighteenth century touched on two vital aspects of history, especially education and economics. A critical examination of these two areas preceded the political dialectics of the days of the independence movement.

Only historical myopia or narrow nationalism—from which the writing of history in our countries unhappily suffers—could deny the close correlation at this time between the economic and educational thought of Spain and its colonies. The schemes and plans, which Spanish rationalists were then devising to overcome Spain's prostration were also adapted to Spanish America. Therefore cosmopolitan ideas, English and French, already perceptible in Creole thought, operated on the common base of a Spanish ideology.

The antithesis in culture and economics that existed then between Spain and its colonies can in no way be compared to the contrast apparent today between the highly advanced and industrialized life of England, for example, and its colonial world in Asia or the Antilles. Speaking figuratively, it is fair to say that Spanish America, in its much larger territory and its proportionately smaller population, did not really augment the economic and scientific backwardness into which the mother country, Spain, had slumped under the last kings of the Habsburg dynasty. Therefore, there was an evident affinity between Feijóo's thoughts on educational reform and Jovellanos's ideas about economic improvements, and the statements of their followers in the colonies about the same subjects. The Madrid of Charles III was the first place to which the Creole turned for knowledge of rationalistic reform. The fact that among the world powers of the time Spain had the least developed capitalistic economy and a deeply rooted medieval way of life, made the cultural and economic situation of the mother country and the colonies much the same. There was, indeed, a general crisis throughout the whole Hispanic organism. A study of Spain's later history in the nineteenth century readily corroborates this statement, for Spain was quite "South American" in the incidence of military strongmen, large landed estates, and a Church politically and economically powerful. It is clear, however, that when the mere longing for reform in the Spain of Charles III was transferred to the colonies, it took on a belligerent tone. This was caused by the peculiarities of the Spanish American situation—the resentment of the natives, the caste feelings, and the ambitions of landed proprietors. Therefore, with a large degree of unity and even of similarity of expression in what the economist Belgrano thought in Buenos Aires and what Manuel de Salas was urging at the same time in Chile, every Creole thinker recognized and identified each other as a part of the common background of the Spanish Enlightenment.

The problem of education comes first in the chronology of eighteenth-century thinking. Such Spanish American rationalists as Baquíjano, Salas, Espejo, Miguel José Sanz, and Francisco José de Caldas had debated this subject at the close of the century. In large measure, their arguments grew out of Feijóo's criticism. In the matter of learning the Hispanic mind of the time had two basic objectives: incorporate into Spanish life the natural sciences and technology present in other European countries, and substitute a clearer and more popular form of expression for the involved and turgid baroque manner. Father Isla had satirized the latter in his *History of the Famous Preacher Friar Gerundio.* Feijóo had built the rationalistic structure of his *Critical Theater* around three or four central ideas. He had asked himself what had taken Spain so far off the main highway of European culture. The following *idola* of national tradition confronted him like phantoms against which he was to fight: (1) the evil of wordy disputes which converted the so-called Spanish "science" of the baroque age into a labyrinthian verbosity devoid of useful content; (2) arguments drawn from scholastic authority that inhibited sound judgment and reason; (3) disdain for experimentation and the observation of nature; and (4) the empty credulity and superstition that hung like Spanish moss on the tree of religious faith. For all these reasons the author of the *Critical Theater* juxtaposed the new and more specific analysis of facts to hollow verbalism, the free use of critical reason to reverence for "authorities," and the neglected natural sciences to purely verbal and syllogistic knowledge. In place of superstition he asked for religious feeling shorn of a nimbus of miracles, needless terror, and silly fables.

When an educated citizen of Venezuela, Miguel José Sanz, indicted colonial education around 1790, he merely carried Feijóo's critical judgments to a logical conclusion. In his address at the inauguration of the Caracas Law School and also in his report, *Public Instruction,* one recognizes Feijóo's empiricism assailing decadent scholasticism in Spanish America. Sanz wanted even the traditionally formalistic discipline of jurisprudence renovated in harmony with the new methods. He wanted the lawyers of colonial Caracas

> to recognize and tell one country from the other through Geography in order to enter into and have a conception of the intricate and complex Common Law of each; learn national customs through History; reflect upon and compare world revolutions; and be aware of the internal and external concerns of his own people, their products, special commercial interests, and their relations to other peoples.

He reiterated with ironic insistence that there was a new kind of learning quite unlike that of "Nebrija's Grammar, Aristotelian Philosophy, Justinian's Institutes, the Curia Philippica, and Gonet's and Larraga's Theology." He coincided with the contemporary rationalists of Spain and Spanish America in still another idea, namely, that nowhere was it so necessarry to exalt manual labor and a respect for the "mechanical and useful arts" as in the Hispanic world because they were so scorned there. This was Manuel de Salas's sole purpose when, a few years after his return to Chile, he set up courses in drawing, mathematics, and chemistry which, in 1797, developed into the Saint Louis Academy, perhaps the earliest college in South America with a modern orientation. Previously Salas had gone to Spain in 1778 to study, and possibly he was introduced into Olavide's circle which was frequented by all studious Spanish Americans during visits to Spain. Like most of his contemporaries Salas had read Campomanes's famous book *Popular Education* (1775) and, on returning home by way of Buenos Aires, he became acquainted with Manuel Belgrano, a fellow enthusiast of books and reforms. Shortly before establishing his academy, Salas had studied English. He therefore was no longer limited to the French works he had brought from Spain but was able to learn the new techniques current in North American educational thought. Manuel de Salas reminds one of Franklin in his double role of thinker and doer.

As if to unify the humanistic thought of the time, busy workers traveled from one colonial province to another keeping in touch with each other through visits, letters, and periodicals. The circle of reformers around Manuel de Salas had been stimulated by José Miguel Lastarria, a colleague of Baquíjano in the academic halls of Lima and an enthusiastic economist and teacher who wrote *An Address for the Protection and Development of Agriculture in Chile* that largely agreed with the views of Salas. Later he would travel in Argentina and to the Paraguayan missions to prepare his lengthy, well-documented treatise on "the eastern colonies on the Paraguay and Plate rivers." Two influences, therefore, converged on Chilean rationalism, one directly from Baquíjano's circle at Lima whose chief interpreter in Santiago was José Miguel Lastarria, and the other the Argentine reform movement that Salas learned about in Buenos Aires through a noble fellowship of ideas with Belgrano. In a similar manner the University of Chuquisaca in Upper Peru would spread its young graduates, imbued with revolutionary fervor, over the southern part of the continent. Among them were Mariano Moreno,

Bernardo Monteaguda, Casimiro Loañeta, and Vicente Pazos Kanki. In Gabriel René Moreno's charming *Last Days of the Colony in Upper Peru*, Chuquisaca is like a Spanish American Salamanca whose inland peace is shattered by those fast-talking students who, at the end of the eighteenth century, came from every corner of Argentina, Chile, and Paraguay, journeying on muleback for thirty or more days.

These meetings of educated representatives from various regions were probably the reason that gave the later revolution for independence its unity of expression and its air of "Spanish American" patriotism that crops up so often in the documents of the time. Had not the friend and confidant of Nariño in Bogotá, Dr. Francisco Javier Eugenio Espejo, dreamed of launching the first insurgent movement in mid-continental Quito? With the visionary intellectualism of the time but without Miranda's genius for plotting, he had thought that the big problem was to bring into agreement all the enlightened persons who could be brought together in the chief Spanish American cities. As an excellent man of letters Espejo was most concerned about a cultural restoration. That his revolutionary motivation was largely educational is clear from his *New Lucianus, or the Alarm Clock of the Gifted* (1779), in which he scoffs at the decadent scholasticism of academic circles in Quito and the convoluted expression of the friars, and from his *First Fruits of Quito Culture* (1791), in which he boldly asserts that colonial education was "a slave education." Was not Espejo himself, a man of mixed Indian and Negro blood, reared from infancy on charity but ennobled, as he himself said, by study—a proof that, however humble a person's status might be, he could be redeemed by enlightened learning?

ECONOMIC CRITICISM

The critical attitude of our American-born rationalists was identified with economics just as was true of Spanish thinkers, notably Campomanes and Jovellanos. Also there was a curious affinity between the economic problems of the mother country and those of its overseas possessions, which explains why such studies as *True Exercise of the*

Arts and Crafts (1785), and *Concerning the Agrarian Law* (1795), both by Jovellanos, found interested readers in the colonies. We have already noted the influence of Campomanes's *Popular Education* on men like Salas and Belgrano. According to Jovellanos, the causes of poverty and industrial backwardness in Spain were similar to those that Spanish American rationalists were beginning to observe in their own provinces, namely: (1) Agricultural property in Spain was considered almost an aristocratic privilege, and the economic welfare of the laboring masses and the true wealth of the country were sacrificed to this feudal concept; as was true in the colonies there was much uncultivated land in Spain. (2) In public and communal lands owners pastured cattle without regard for any other return. (3) The excessive amount of amortized property (entailed estates and Church lands) prevented redistribution into small holdings and a free economy. "Spanish legislation," noted the author of *The Agrarian Law*, "facilitated land accumulation within the same class and by corporations. Most of the property in Castile belonged to churches and monasteries whose originally modest endowments have become immense." (4) This monopolistic system, exemplified by the *mesta* or cattle-raisers' union in Castile, and the exclusive possession of property by the idle rich who neglected or did not cultivate it regularly, caused the exodus of the landless, unemployed farmer to the cities where he turned to mendicancy and crime. Added to, and as an outgrowth of, such stagnation was the ignorance of the peasant who preserved the crudest and most outworn agricultural methods used in Europe.

Basically, the picture drawn by Jovellanos coincides with that by Manuel de Salas in his *State of Agriculture, Industry, and Commerce in the Kingdom of Chile,* and by Belgrano in his *General Means of Encouraging Agriculture, Accelerating Industry, and Protecting Trade in an Agricultural Country,* both written in 1790. These two writers stress the shocking inequality in colonial economic life, the few proprietors, the excessive and contradictory taxation, the trade monopoly, the amortized wealth, and the dreary monotony and poverty of the great masses of Indians and mixed elements. Later Humboldt drew a striking parallel in his *Essay on New Spain* between the social conditions of that viceroyalty and the vast, then semibarbarian Russian empire. He compared the landed proprietors of Mexico with the Slav boyars, while the splendor and refinement of the upper classes in both Mexico and Russia contrasted with the almost prehistoric way of life of the rural masses.

What was the remedy for this situation? Both Spanish and Spanish American rationalists at the close of the eighteenth century were taking deep draughts from Adam Smith's *Wealth of Nations,* which was a kind of Bible of the new age and the cherished baptismal certificate of liberal economics. Like Rousseau's *Social Contract,* it was one of those works that determine an era. Familiar already to men such as Cabarrús and Campomanes, this English work became enormously popular in Spain because of a translation which Carlos Martínez de Irujo published in Madrid in 1792 made from a French summary written by the Marquis de Condorcet. Freedom of trade, an automatic reflex on the part of the eager Creole, now made its appearance wrapped in the mantle of scientific truth. Would not all economic problems of Spanish America be solved by freedom of trade and instruction in the "useful arts and crafts"? We find an immediate echo of this line of thought in public papers such as the *Address of the Farmers of Buenos Aires,* possibly inspired by Belgrano and presented to the viceroy in 1793. This is presumably the first official document in which the Creole's economic consciousness is stated in a forthright and emphatic manner. It preceded by almost twenty years another *Address of the Planters of the River Plate* which Mariano Moreno wrote in 1810 when the revolutionary spirit of the Creole came to maturity. The enthusiastic "farmers" of 1793 declared:

> It is well known that the fruits of the land are the true wealth of a country, and upon them depends the continuity and the increase of peoples and their sovereign. The love of gain is the keenest incentive for men to work, to foster industry, and to carry out the hardest undertakings. This desire which brings abundance should not be dulled but sharpened by a freedom compatible with justice and public utility.

If there was a bit of capitalistic greed in that *Address of the Farmers,* if the "love of gain" became a new social faith, if it well expressed the Creole proprietor's longing for new markets and to produce and earn more, Belgrano and Salas were already endowing the slogan "economic freedom" with a more democratic meaning. In Chile, Salas was explaining that "the lack of commercial freedom limited production and cramped industry by depriving inhabitants of jobs." And Belgrano was declaring that "the nearer a state is to complete liberty in its internal and external trade, the nearer it is to a steady prosperity. If it is fettered, its steps toward prosperity are slow and far apart."

The Creole's thought during the last days of the eighteenth century was that change is necessary for improvement. The old values that until then had supported the edifice of Spanish overseas possessions were disintegrating and now ways and means to replace them were eagerly sought. In Buenos Aires, Mexico City, Bogotá, Quito, or Caracas the attitude was the same, and it would be both tedious and superfluous to relate in detail how the same words and utopian ideas were repeated all over the continent. In the first issue of his *First Fruits of Quito's Culture* Francisco Javier Eugenio Espejo published in lyric terms a fervent invitation to change: "We are in the darkest and farthermost corner of the world where but a few refracted rays of the vast light that illumines the privileged regions reach us; we are without books, tools, means, and instructors to show us the elements of many subjects and to teach us the way to learn them."

THE DREAM OF POLITICAL FREEDOM. THE DAWN OF THE REVOLUTION

From an increasingly realistic social criticism other paths were leading to a full consciousness of political freedom itself. To trace the thermometric fluctuations of the independence idea before 1800 nothing is so instructive as volumes 14 and 15 of Francisco de Miranda's personal *Archive*. There the celebrated Venezuelan conspirator, who had a curious penchant for the oddest records, collected news items, jottings, letters, and reports on what he had heard, thought, seen, or read between 1770 and 1796.

Volume 15 opens with a printed brochure dated 1770 in which a French adventurer, Marquis D'Aubarede, tried to interest England in his project for setting up a republic in Mexico. Miranda brought lengthy memoranda to his interviews to convince the British minister Pitt and his London friends whose support was needed for the Venezuelan's revolutionary schemes. These data included estimates of the populations of the various Spanish colonies, the number of people that the latter could support, the military forces with which Spain garrisoned its overseas possessions, and the economic resources of these territories. With much emotion he pointed out the revolutionary discontent implicit in the uprisings of Tupac Amaru and of the Socorro commoners in 1781. He produced a letter, dated in 1783, in which such wealthy and reputable gentlemen of Caracas as Juan Vicente Bolívar, Martín Tobar, and the Marquis of Mejares thought of Miranda himself as the strongman of a future revolution. In a 1790 memorandum to Pitt he declared that "Spain blinds the mental eyes of Spanish Americans so as to keep them submissive." And finally, his fellow plotter, the former Jesuit Juan Bautista Vizcardo y Guzmán, seized the third centenary of the discovery of America as a symbolic occasion to launch his explosive *Letter to Spanish Americans*.

No piece of writing was so widely disseminated as propaganda as this work of an impassioned friar. It was translated into French and printed in Philadelphia, and it received the accolade of an English version in the respected *Edinburgh Gazette*. Miranda later distributed many copies of it on the occasion of his first ill-fated expedition to northern South America in 1806. Priests, inquisitors, and royal officials hunted down this pamphlet as they would the most dangerous pirates. Historically it may be regarded as the earliest proclamation of the "revolution," for it was the best synthesis of the Creoles' aspirations in their struggle against the Spanish monarchy, namely: the dream of political and economic freedom, the rehabilitation and idealization of the Indian as the legitimate and despoiled owner of the soil, the theory of popular sovereignty, and the new mysticism of nationalism. Vizcardo y Guzmán's powerful and ringing words later appeared in variations in the first great documents of the war

for independence such as those of the Chilean friar Camilo Henríquez, or in *The Report of Wrongs Suffered*, written by the heroic
Colombian Camilo Torres. Along with Pozo y Sucre and Salas, self-
appointed Spanish American delegates, Miranda had signed an independence pact. And this arch-Venezuelan conspirator who, during
his intermittent periods of residence in Paris and London, had introduced his guests to secret lodges organized under his inspiration, the
Societies of Gentlemen Rationalists, the Great American Assembly,
or Lautaro Lodge, regarded Vizcardo y Guzmán as a propaganda
minister. No one stated Spanish American rancor more expressively.
The commemoration of the three hundredth anniversary of the discovery of America, "the most memorable event in the annals of mankind," moved him to make a rapid rundown of the Spanish colonial
regime. He declared:

> The mother country, has kept us apart from the world and
> has abducted us from all contact with the rest of the human
> species. On top of this usurpation of our personal freedom, it
> has added the no less harmful and vexatious seizure of our
> property. Since men first lived together in communities for
> mutual benefit we are the only ones in the world whom a
> government forces to pay the most for necessities while obliging
> us to sell products of our labor at the lowest price. We are
> hermetically sealed off like a city under siege to make this
> violent procedure produce its fullest effect.

After dwelling on the abuses of the monopolistic system imposed
on the colonial economy, he applied a theory of freedom to the
Spanish American revolution which seems to bring into harmony
both Rousseau and the theologians of the scholastic era. "Unques-
tionably the bedrock of any human community, whatever its political organization, is the preservation of natural rights, above all the
preservation of personal freedom and private property. We are compelled," he added, "to reclaim our God-given rights, precious rights
that we have no power to alienate and of which we can not be de-
prived without being guilty of crime. Can a man, perchance, re-
nounce his reason? Well, his personal freedom is no less his birth-
right."

From 1792 to 1800, when Vizcardo y Guzmán's letter was written and circulated, ideas in Spanish America were changing into realities. One day in 1794 a prosperous and educated landowner of Bogotá, Antonio de Nariño, received as the gift of a friend a copy of the *Histoire d'Assemblée Constituante* by Salart de Monjoie, which recounts the first stages of the French Revolution before the Jacobin terror. When Nariño was not riding on horseback around his splendid estate situated on the grassy plains near Bogotá he often liked to shut himself up in his library containing 6,000 volumes— possibly the largest private collection of books in the viceroyalty— or he discussed with his associates what banned authors had said. One of Nariño's pleasures was to print the more appealing ideas that he extracted from his books on a small hand press and present copies to his friends. Franklin's portrait and important quotations from Voltaire, Rousseau, and Montesquieu adorned the walls of his study. That is how the youthful citizen of Bogotá came to see the seventeen articles of the *Declaration of the Rights of Man and of the Citizen* in Salart de Monjoie's bulky volume. Excited by these statements he translated them into Spanish and, in the conventlike silence of the city, worked at his secret hand press printing loose-sheet copies by the hundreds. They went to the remotest cities of the viceroyalty, Popayán and Quito, Cartagena and Caracas, without the name of the translator and printer. His Quito friend and correspondent, Francisco Javier Eugenio Espejo, had been jailed by the Spanish government at the time in the Ecuadorean city for the crime of participation in a plot that was more literary than real. When the author of the subversive translation was ascertained, he was promptly imprisoned, his property confiscated, and he was sent a prisoner to Spain. Thus began the long, heroic trajectory of one of the noblest lives to be tested by alien persecution that Spanish America has produced. "The seventeen articles of the Rights of Man cost me more than that number of years of imprisonment and persecution," the great Colombian precursor of independence, old and ill, declared shortly before his death. But the wide repercussions of his message indicate how well he had aimed at his target and that he spread the words that the people were waiting for. Magistrates and police agents from the Ecuadorean Andes to the mountain range along the Caribbean were busy rounding up circulating copies. Several years later a clergyman, José Cortés de Madariaga, a former correspondent of Miranda and ardently revolutionary in his sentiments, stopped in the city of Mérida while en route from Caracas to Bogotá. There he read a pastoral letter of the local bishop posted on the cathedral wall excommunicating any of his flock with a copy of the *Rights of Man* in his possession. With his own hands this rebellious curate, later a popular leader and orator in behalf of the uprising at Caracas in 1810, angrily tore down the reactionary ecclesiastical decree.

In the decade 1790–1800 the French Revolution came to the Spanish Americans directly and also by way of Spain. A group of Spanish teachers—Juan Bautista Picornell, Manuel Cortés de Campomanes, and Sebastián Andrés—steeped in the writings of Rousseau and with a blind faith in the efficacy of ideas, concocted the so-called San Blas conspiracy in Spain, which was the earliest dream of setting up a democratic Hispanic republic. When these plotters, acting under the influence of French ideas, were discovered and taken prisoner, they were shipped off to the dungeons of La Guaira on the distant shores of the Caribbean. But La Guaira was precisely one of the places in Spanish America most completely infected by the rising spirit of agitation, for it was a port of call of the Basque ships that exported the precious cacao of Caracas. It was also close to the English, French, and Dutch Antilles that were active smuggling centers both of goods and subversive ideas.

Venezuela was enjoying exceptional prosperity at that time. In their social gatherings its planters and magnates, the so-called "marquises of cacao and tobacco," talked about the necessity of freeing themselves from the restrictive tutelage of the Spanish state. The desire of these aristocrats to be stronger and manage their own affairs independently was not appreciably weakened by any fear of the "castes," the colored and mixed elements, who were feeling the lure of the new revolutionary ideal of *egalité*.

At that time, one bold-minded mulatto, Chirino, of Coro, who had completed his political education in the Antilles and had witnessed the upheavals in Haiti, was turning over in his mind the idea of subverting the "castes" not only against the Spanish government but also against the irritating privileges enjoyed by the Creole aristocracy. Besides, Spanish political prisoners at La Guaira had received numerous visitors in their cells and they had managed to acquire books and pamphlets with the acquiescence of benevolent jailers. Thus they stimulated still another Venezuelan conspiracy, the principal agents of which were Manuel Gual and José María España. In 1797 Gual was about fifty years old, a childhood playmate of Francisco de Miranda, an avid reader of pamphlets, and a former captain of the military service unhappy in his retirement and eager for a bigger job and more glory. España, a modest magistrate in the town of Macuto, rather curiously reminds one of Pedro Crespo, the mayor in Calderón's play. His faith and mystical sense of justice were completely Spanish. When the plot was uncovered on July 13, 1797, the two Spaniards, Picornell and Campomanes, fled to Trinidad, and from that asylum Gual wrote to Miranda trying to hurry the latter's plans. The magistrate of Macuto, however, was unable to save himself—after a harsh imprisonment he yielded his head to the executioner with classic stoicism. Nevertheless, despite cruel persecution by the Captain-General of Venezuela, Guevara y Vasconcelos, revolutionary pamphlets and letters by the indefatigable conspirator Francisco de Miranda, continued to reach those shores.

The departure of the adolescent Simón Bolívar on January 19, 1799, aboard the *San Ildefonso* to study in Europe, is symbolic. He had already had the instruction of three of the most extraordinary teachers that Venezuela had to offer at that time. They were Licentiate Sanz, a critic of colonial education, young Andrés Bello who, before he was twenty years old, was the most accomplished Latinist and acute interpreter of classic and modern literature in the captaincy-general of Venezuela and, finally, the strange Simón Rodríguez, a practicing follower of Rousseau and wholehearted foe of every form of tyranny, whether of family, Church, or state. In his letters, the future emancipator was still quite deficient in matters of spelling, but the boldness and energy with which he spoke and acted more than compensated for this shortcoming. The *San Ildefonso* made long stops in ports along its roundabout course which allowed passengers to land at Vera Cruz and to travel up to the viceregal capital, and in Mexico City the adolescent Simón Bolívar got into a hot dispute at an aristocratic gathering when he defended the recent insurrection of his countrymen Gual and España.

Storm-ridden Europe, its thrones collapsing, its royalty in flight, its twenty-five-year-old generals and its incipient romanticism, visible in personal exploits before it was in literature, was to afford young Bolívar ample study and preparation for his forthcoming revolutionary career. The colonial era was coming to an end and, in that late afternoon of the eighteenth century, the coming agitation and confusion of the revolution were already in sight.

The colonial order of castes and social classes was soon to break up and bring forth striking personalities in the early leaders and strongmen. No one yet knew who they would be, nor how a young aristocrat of Caracas would be transformed into the chief of semi-nomadic plainsmen, nor how a modest officer from the most obscure part of the viceroyalty of Rio de la Plata would lead the wild gauchos of the Argentine pampas to distant Peru; nor yet again how a village curate of Mexico, who planted mulberry trees by day and translated French by night, would be the first to take up the standard of independence in that country, nor how a rejected, illegitimate son, still unable to sign himself Bernardo O'Higgins, whom Miranda had introduced into the early secret orders of conspirators, would encourage the Chilean revolution contrary to the aristocratic prejudices and the repugnance of the "best families."

Characteristic of the spiritual and intellectual climate of those days was the consciousness of a common destiny for all Hispanic America, which later we unhappily lost. Miranda called his friends and correspondents from Mexico City to Buenos Aires his fellow countrymen. And so it was that Madariaga, a Chilean, went to Caracas to fight for the revolution, while a Guatemalan named Irisarri was one of the cleverest pamphleteers for independence in Santigao de Chile. Then the great idea and the duty that lay ahead knew no boundaries.

Selected Bibliography

Arroyo, Anita. *Razón y Pasión de Sor Juana*. Mexico City: Porrúa y Obregon, 1952.

Barth, Pius J. *Franciscan Education and the Social Order in Spanish North America (1502–1821)*. Chicago: University of Chicago Press, 1945.

Bolton, Herbert E. *Coronado, Knight of Pueblos and Plains*. New York: Whittlesey, 1945.

——. *Rim of Christendom*. New York: Russell, 1960.

Borah, Woodrow. *New Spain's Century of Depression*. Berkeley and Los Angeles: University of California Publications in Ibero-Americana, No. 35, 1951.

Bourne, E. G. *Spain in America, 1450–1580*. New York: 1904.

Braden, Charles S. *Religious Aspects of the Conquest of Mexico*. Durham, North Carolina: Duke University Press, 1930.

Conway, G. R. G. (ed.). *Friar Francisco Naranjo and the Old University of Mexico*. Mexico City: Gante Press, 1939.

Crow, John A. *The Epic of Latin America*. Garden City, New York: Doubleday, 1946.

Chapman, Charles E. *Colonial Hispanic America: A History*. New York: Macmillan, 1933, 1940.

Cunningham-Graham, R. B. *A Vanished Arcadia: Being Some Account of the Jesuits in Paraguay, 1607–1767*. New York: 1924.

Díaz del Castillo, Bernal. *The Discovery and Conquest of Mexico*. Many editions.

Diffie, Bailey W. *Latin American Civilization: Colonial Period*. Harrisburg, Pennsylvania: Stackpole, 1945.

Fisher, Lillian E. *Viceregal Administration in the Spanish Colonies*. Berkeley: University of California Publicatons in History, Vol. 15, 1926.

——. *The Background of the Revolution for Mexican Independence*. Boston: 1934.

Friedrich, Carl J. *The Age of the Baroque, 1610–1660*. New York: Harper, 1952.

González Obregón, Luis. *The Streets of Mexico*. Trans. by B. C. Wagner. San Francisco: G. Fields, 1937.

Hamilton, Earl J. *American Treasure and the Rise of Capitalism, 1500–1700*. London: 1929.

———. *American Treasure and the Price Revolution in Spain, 1501–1650*. Cambridge, Mass.: Harvard University Press, 1934.

Hanke, Lewis. *The Spanish Struggle for Justice*. Philadelphia: University of Pennsylvania Press, 1949.

Haring, Clarence H. *The Spanish Empire in America*. New York: Oxford University Press, 1947.

Henríquez Ureña, Pedro. *Literary Currents in Hispanic America*. Cambridge, Mass.: Harvard University Press, 1945.

Herr, Richard. *The Eighteenth-century Revolution in Spain*. Princeton University Press, 1958.

Humboldt, Alexander von. *Political Essay on the Kingdom of New Spain*. London: 1811–1822. 4 vols.

———. *Personal Narrative of Travels to the Equinoctial Regions of the New Continent during the Years 1799–1804*. London: 1814–1829. 7 vols.

Jacobsen, J. V. *Educational Foundations of the Jesuits in Sixteenth-century New Spain*. Berkeley: University of California Press, 1938.

Jane, Cecil. *Liberty and Despotism in Spanish America*. Oxford: 1929.

Joyce, Thomas. *South American Archeology*. London: 1912.

———. *Central American Archeology*. London: 1916.

———. *Mexican Archeology*. London: 1914.

———. *Maya and Mexican Art*. London: 1927.

Kelemen, Pál. *Baroque and Rococo in Latin America*. New York: Macmillan, 1951.

Kirkpatrick, F. A. *The Spanish Conquistadors*. New York: 1934.

Kolb, Glen L. *Juan del Valle Caviedes. A Study of Life, Times and Poetry*. New London: Connecticut College, 1959.

Lanning, John Tate. *Academic Culture in the Spanish Colonies*. New York: Oxford University Press, 1940.

———. *The University in the Kingdom of Guatemala*. Ithaca, New York: Cornell University Press, 1955.

———. *The Eighteenth-century Enlightenment in the University of San Carlos de Guatemala*. Ithaca, New York: Cornell University Press, 1956.

Lea, Charles H. *The Inquisition in the Spanish Dependencies*. New York: 1908.

Lehmann, Walter. *The Art of Old Peru*. London: 1924.

Leonard, Irving A. *Don Carlos de Sigüenza y Góngora, a Mexican Savant of the Seventeenth Century.* Berkeley: University of California Publications in History, Vol. 18, 1929.

———. *The Spanish Approach to Pensacola, 1689–1693.* Albuquerque: The Quivira Society, 1939.

———. *Books of the Brave: Being an Account of Books and Men in the Spanish Conquest and Settlement of the Sixteenth Century New World.* Cambridge, Mass.: Harvard University Press, 1949.

———. *Baroque Times in Old Mexico.* Ann Arbor: University of Michigan Press, 1959.

Madariaga, Salvador de. *The Rise of the Spanish American Empire.* New York: Macmillan, 1947.

———. *The Fall of the Spanish American Empire.* London: Hollis and Carter, 1947.

Means, Philip A. *Ancient Civilization of the Andes.* New York: 1931.

———. *The Fall of the Inca Empire.* New York: 1932.

Morley, S. G. *The Ancient Maya.* Stanford University Press, 1947; revised 1956.

Morris, J. Bayard. *Hernando Cortes: Five Letters.* London: 1928; New York: 1929.

Moses, Bernard. *Spanish Colonial Literature in South America.* London–New York: 1922.

———. *The Intellectual Background of the Revolution in South America, 1810–1824.* New York: 1926.

Motten, C. G. *Mexican Silver and the Enlightenment.* Philadelphia; University of Pennsylvania Press, 1950.

Newton, A. P. (ed.). *Thomas Gage, The English-American: A New Survey of the West Indies, 1648.* Many editions.

Prescott, William H. *Conquest of Mexico.* Many editions.

———. *Conquest of Peru.* Many editions.

Priestley, Herbert I. *José de Gálvez, Visitor-General of New Spain (1765–1771).* Berkeley: University of California Publications in History, Vol. 5, 1916; Berkeley: University of California Press, 1916.

Rodríguez Freile, J. *The Conquest of New Granada.* A translation by William C. Atkinson of *El Carnero.* London: Folio Society, 1961.

Robertson, William S. *Life of Miranda.* Chapel Hill: University of North Carolina Press, 1929. 2 vols.

Schurz, William L. *The Manila Galleon.* New York: Dutton, 1959.

———. *This New World.* New York: Dutton, 1959.

Shafer, R. J. *The Economic Societies in the Spanish World, 1763–1821.* Syracuse, New York: Syracuse University Press, 1958.

Simpson, Lesley B. *The Encomienda in New Spain: The Beginning of Spanish Mexico.* Berkeley and Los Angeles: University of California Press, 1950.

——. *Studies in the Administration of the Indians in New Spain: III, The Repartimiento System of Forced Native Labor in New Spain and Guatemala.* Berkeley: University of California Publications in Ibero-Americana, No. 13, 1938.

Spinden, H. J. *Ancient Civilizations of Mexico and Central America.* New York: 1928.

Tannenbaum, Frank. *Slave and Citizen. The Negro in the Americas.* New York: Knopf, 1947.

Thompson, J. Eric. *Mexico before Cortez.* New York: 1933.

——. *The Civilization of the Mayas.* Chicago: Field Museum of Natural History, 1936.

Thorning, Joseph F. *Miranda, World Citizen.* Gainesville: University of Florida Press, 1952.

Vaillant, George C. *The Aztecs of Mexico.* Baltimore: Pelican Books, 1950.

Varner, J. G. and J. J. (trans.). *The Florida of the Inca.* Austin: University of Texas Press, 1951.

Wethey, Harold E. *Colonial Architecture and Sculpture in Peru.* Cambridge, Mass.: Harvard University Press, 1949.

Whitaker, Arthur P. (ed.). *Latin America and the Enlightenment.* 2d ed., Ithaca, New York: Cornell University Press (Great Seal Books), 1961.

Wilgus, A. Curtis (ed.). *Colonial Hispanic America.* Washington, D.C.: 1936.

Wolf, A. *History of Science, Technology, and Philosophy in the Sixteenth and Seventeenth Centuries.* New York: 1935.

Index

Charles V, 24, 32, 40
Chart of the Ecuadorean Territory, by Maldonado, 131
chavín art, 3
Chibcha kingdoms, 6
Chimu culture, 5, 6
Chirino of Coro: plots racial revolt, 173–174
Cholula, 2, 62
Christian Rule, by Bishop Zumárraga: quoted, 61
Chronicle of Brazil, by Vasconcelos, 126
Chronicle of 1810, by Amunátegui, 130
church, 74, 75, 77
Cinteotl, god of maize, 2
Cipac, Marcos, Indian painter, 58
Claver, Pedro, protector of slaves, 119, 120
Clavijero, Francisco Xavier, historian, 116, 133, 142; quoted, 137–139
Coatlicue, Aztec goddess, 9
Colloquies, by Pérez Ramírez, 67
Colombia, x, 21, 46, 54, 70, 71, 76, 94, 117, 125, 132, 145, 158, 161; *comunero* revolt, 136, 170
Colombian Literature, by Gómez Restrepo, 118
colonial journalism, 159–161
Columbia University, xi, xiii, xiv
Columbus, Diego, 42, 43
Coming of the Messiah in Glory . . ., by Lacunza, 118–119
Compendium . . . of the Kingdom of Chile, by Molina, 132
conceptismo, 88
Conquest of Mexico, by Solís, 123
Copacabana, 64
Corpus Christi, 2, 63, 64, 65
Cortés, Hernán, 36, 37, 44, 48; quoted, 19, 31, 34–35; meets Franciscans, 49
Cortés, Martín, son of Hernán, 20
Cortés, Martín, cosmographer, 106

Cortés de Campomanes, Manuel, 173, 174
Cortés de Madariaga, José, 173
Counter Reformation, 38, 90, 92, 106, 107, 147
Crisis of the European Conscience, by Paul Hazard, 130
Cristiad, The, by Hojeda, 116
Critical Theater, by Benito Feijóo, 163–164
Crucible of Disillusionment, by Nieremberg, 90
Cuauhtémoc, 11, 44
Cueva, Juan de la, poet, 54
Cuicuilco, 2
culteranismo, 88
Curious Account of Life, Laws, Customs and Rites of the Indians, by Tomás de Ortiz, 46
Cuzco, 18, 64, 65, 94, 136

Darío, Rubén, poet, 87
De Potestate Ecclesiae, by Father Vitoria, 40
Declaration of the Rights of the Indians: quoted, 48
Díaz de Gamarra, Benito de, rationalist, 127–128, 149
Díaz del Castillo, Bernal: quoted 23–24, 26
Díaz Moreno, conqueror in Venezuela, 36
Discourse in Praise of Poetry, 97
Disputationum theologicarum . . ., by Peñafiel, 115
Dominicans, 50, 57, 74, 77, 124
drama, liturgical, 63–67
Due Antichi Monumenti di Architettura Messicana, by P. J. Márquez, 139
Durán, Diego, chronicler, 8, 14, 58, 60; quoted, 12

Echave, Francisco, writer, 120
Economic Society of Friends of the Country, 145, 149
Ecuador, 1, 2, 3, 94, 132, 157